The Emotionally Intelligent Office

20 Key Emotional Skills for the Workplace

D0680747

The Emotionally Intelligent Office

20 Key Emotional Skills for the Workplace

The School of Life

Published in 2018 by The School of Life
70 Marchmont Street, London WC1N 1AB

Copyright © The School of Life 2018

Designed and typeset by Marcia Mihotich

Printed in Belgium by Graphius

A proportion of this book has appeared online at
thebookoflife.org

Every effort has been made to contact the copyright holders
of the material reproduced in this book. If any have been
inadvertently overlooked, the publisher will be pleased to
make restitution at the earliest opportunity.

The School of Life offers programmes, publications and
services to assist modern individuals in their quest to live more
engaged and meaningful lives. We've also developed a collection
of content-rich, design-led retail products to promote useful
insights and ideas from culture.

www.theschooloflife.com

ISBN 978-0-9957535-8-7

10 9 8 7 6 5 4 3 2 1

Contents

1 Adaptability	2 Calm
3 Charm	4 Communication
5 Confidence	6 Creativity
7 Decisiveness	8 Diplomacy
9 Effectiveness	10 Eloquence

11 Empathy

12 Entrepreneurship

13 Innovation

14 Leadership

15 Objectivity

16 Playfulness

17 Purpose

18 Resilience

19 Self-awareness

20 Supportiveness

Introduction

A good business education teaches us a host of vital skills: how to navigate a balance sheet, analyse competitors, negotiate contracts, market and sell. But when we reach the office, we may be confronted by other, less familiar, kinds of challenges: the person at the desk opposite us with the charming manner who enthusiastically agrees with whomever they're speaking to yet harbours a range of toxic reservations and privately pursues their own unstated agenda; the person who responds to polite criticism or well-meaning feedback with immediate hurt and fury; the person who follows orders dutifully but cannot generate an original vision or initiative; the person who manifests a rivalrous and factional nature...

In days gone by, when work only required people to turn a boat swiftly starboard, push coal trolleys up a hill, or increase the rate of production at a blast furnace, psychological dynamics were of negligible economic importance or interest. A worker could feel underappreciated, bullied and belittled and still perform their role perfectly. Even when they hated the supervisor and there were communication issues in the team, they could operate the brick making machine at optimal speed. If the head gardener had a macho streak, the men watering in the greenhouses or pruning in the orchard could not imagine they would work for anyone much better. Emotional distress could be ignored.

Yet many of us now labour with our minds (and souls) far more than with our bodies. Our work requires from us continuous interaction, creativity, personal service and intellectual concentration, and is therefore susceptible to the prevailing emotional atmosphere.

The quality of our efforts has grown reliant on tricky, elusive fare: a sense of meaning, respect, inner fulfilment, encouragement and a spirit close to friendship. A wounding comment or curt interaction may ruin the productive potential of an afternoon. Profitability has grown reliant on feelings.

So peculiar and awkward is this phenomenon, it is tempting to deny that it might even exist. It would be much easier if workers could remain at all times 'professional' – that is, logical, efficient, straightforward, insensitive to mild insult, responsive to brute command and uninclined to mental breakdown. We are under pressure to forget the difficult truth that we know from personal life: that humans are exhaustingly complex, unpredictable and fragile.

Our desire to assume that the workplace is emotionally simpler than it really is has been partly sustained by its long-standing neglect at the hands of culture. Films, novels and art dealing with the emotional aspects of office life have been in a minority, and this gap has hampered our ability to understand the significance of our real experiences at work.

For the last two hundred years, the meaning of our lives has been tightly connected with love and work, yet the arts have been very selective about which of these two ideals they have looked at. They have engaged intimately with love, charting its key moments and giving us a language with which to explore its yearnings and griefs. Conversely, work has been almost entirely ignored.

If a visiting Martian were asked to assess human priorities on the evidence of the plots of novels alone, it might be astonished to learn that humans do not spend all their time falling in and out of love (and occasionally murdering one another), but devote a predominant share of their energies to going to the office. Precious little of the reality of our lives at work makes it onto the page or screen, the stated reason being that it would be boring; the deeper reason being that it requires an uncommon amount of genius to tease out the latent interest and drama of workplace dynamics. But we collectively pay a price for this silence: without art, our feelings go by unattended and we lack a sufficiently rich language with which to interpret ourselves.

Insofar as culture has taken us to work, it has been to the studio, and to the excitements and sorrows of the creative artist, about which we know a great deal. In the 19th century, the studio became the quintessential image of the place of work, often characterised by sloping ceilings, large windows, a view over neighbouring rooftops, sparse furniture, the smell of turpentine, messy tables covered in tubes of paint and half-finished masterpieces propped against the walls. There was an additional factor that particularly enticed the collective imagination: the studio was a place of solitude. Here the artist could carry out projects without asking anyone's permission or approval. He or she was free of one of the greatest sources of agitation of modern life: other people.

Our cultural representation of work has taken us perilously far from a just appreciation and understanding of what we ourselves are most likely to face in our jobs. We are constantly invited to read interviews with singers and novelists, but we seldom eavesdrop on the tensions inside teams of warehouse support staff responsible for

Depictions of working life in
the 19th century often included
an idealised view of the artist
working in glorious solitude.
__Carl Friedrich H. Werner,
The Artist's Studio, Venice, 1855.

the distribution of homeware products. Therefore, we fail to develop an appropriate sympathy for the skills and qualities of mind that will help to make our collaborations tolerable and successful.

In relation to artistic work, we have been carefully educated as to some of the challenges involved in creating finished products by the prestige accorded to artists' sketches. These show us the prevarications, false starts and sheer resilience routinely exacted by art. This has implicitly taught us to relinquish impatience and unhelpful perfectionism when we in turn sit down to create.

However, we lack the equivalent of a sketch for most working lives. We encounter the fruits of non-artistic labour without the surrounding stories and images of their genesis. We look at a pristine piece of technology, a contract, a car or a holiday company without learning of the background agonies that went into its creation: the late nights, the stubborn boss, the indecisive sales director, the rivalries and setbacks. Therefore, when we hit difficulties in our working lives, we're inclined to panic and believe that something has gone particularly wrong for us.

When we work alone, we constantly undertake complicated manoeuvres in our minds. If we could listen in to our inner monologue as we wrote, painted or took photos, it would comprise a series of baffling telegraphic assertions, suggestions and jumbled words: 'No, yes. Come on! Ah, nearly, nononno no, back... OK, got it, got it... No. Yes. That's fine. Now this...'

Collaborations in office contexts require just as many stages and revisions, but these have to be made explicit and shared

Artists' sketches give us an appreciation of the behind-the-scenes labour that goes into producing works of art – a view we tend to lack in relation to other fields of work.
__Raphael, *Head of Saint Catherine and Sketches of Cupids*, c. 1507–8.

among a group. The process is liable to appear cumbersome and laboured. However, the techniques themselves are not in any way unworthy or superfluous. Compromise, scheduling, sitting through meetings, offering clarity, carefully listening before an objection is raised, mastering one's ego, not taking offence where none was intended, learning to see what might be good about an idea that we didn't originate: all of these moves deserve an as yet unexplored prestige and deference.

The central problem of colleagues is that they are not you. To grasp why this matters so much, we need to contemplate the condition of the baby who does not realise that its mother is a separate being. Only after a long and difficult process of development can a child realise that a parent is a distinct individual with a life and history outside their relationship to their child – and it may be the work of a lifetime to gradually accept that this is the case.

We largely model our sense of what other people are like, and of what might be going on in their heads, on our experience of ourselves. We find it difficult to imagine that others might not be much like us. Other people have different skills, different weaknesses, different motives and different fears. It is as if the human brain did not evolve with the need to address this problem. For most of the time that human beings have existed, it may have been sufficient – for individual and group survival – to operate with very limited interest in how other people's minds work.

In the office, other people are out of our control, yet we need their assistance in performing delicate, complicated tasks. Others cannot by instinct alone understand what you need; they don't share your vision, their interests do not perfectly align with yours. It is difficult to transform our own inner convictions, attitudes and motives into material that makes sense to other people – and it is not really our fault if we lack the necessary skills to do so. Of course, it would be nicer if we could work alone, but the rationale of offices lies in the unavoidable fact that a huge range of commercial and administrative tasks cannot be undertaken by solitary individuals. Sadly, you can't run an airline or operate a distribution centre on your own.

We are ultimately frustrated with our colleagues not only because collaboration is difficult, but because it is much more difficult than we suppose it should be. Here, the fault lies not so much with us as with a background culture that fails to correctly prime us with appropriate attitudes of patience and awe for the sorrows and pleasures of the office.

There is one part of culture that has, inadvertently, thought a lot about office life. Although ostensibly limiting itself to issues of private (especially sexual and romantic) life, psychoanalysis has also shed light on the dynamics of the world of work. It has given us a set of highly transferable theories that illuminate not only the bedroom and the nursery but also much of what happens at the conference table, the performance review and the sales meeting.

At the core of the psychoanalytic worldview is a story about childhood: home is where we originated and where, in many ways, we remain, especially insofar as we are uninclined to give our past the thought it requires. The early years were periods of acute vulnerability that have shaped and will continue to dominate adult behaviour. The most basic truth about our identities is that we were, at first, utterly at the mercy of the prevailing environment. We could not properly move, speak, control or contain ourselves; we could not calm ourselves down or recover our equilibrium. We had no choice about who to direct our feelings towards and no way to defend ourselves adequately against what injured us. We could not even string thoughts together, needing the language eventually lent to us by others to begin to interpret our requirements. Even in the most benign of circumstances, with only the best intentions at play, the possibilities for warps and distortions were enormous. Few of us came through unscathed.

Psychoanalysis explains that what we experienced in those early years now moulds the expectations with which we approach the people and situations of our adult lives. What we feel we're owed, how we speak to ourselves, our sense of how our hopes may turn out – all are extrapolations from experiences and relationships of a distant past whose particulars we may find it hard to recall.

A lot of our difficulties at work stem from these unknown psychological legacies. What we don't see on every CV, alongside qualifications and technical experience, is the litany of psychological entanglements we bring along, uninvited, to the workstation and the meeting room. Ten people around a table means ten different early households, at least twenty different carers and book-length psychological narratives as convoluted as they are generally unknown and unread.

These histories interfere with our ability to respond with lucidity, courage and soberness to the present. We interpret reality

_____ What we don't see on every CV is the litany of psychological entanglements we bring along, uninvited, to the workstation and the meeting room.

with a bias that twists the available evidence according to narratives that feel familiar but may be untrue and unhelpful to who and what is actually before us. Psychoanalysis calls this imposition of a past assumption onto present reality a transference. This is a phenomenon whereby a situation in the here and now elicits from us a response – generally in some way exaggerated, extreme, intense or rigid – that was cobbled together in childhood to meet a threat that we were at that time too inexperienced to cope with adequately, and that the present does not now wholly warrant.

The task of growing up is to realise what exaggerated dynamics we may bring to situations and to monitor ourselves more accurately and more critically so as to improve our capacity to judge and act on situations with greater fairness and neutrality. But maturity also means being aware of how fragile true maturity will always be – and therefore what a bizarre brew of neuroses, excitements and troubles a typical day at the office will generate.

What follow are twenty emotional skills designed to help us respond with as much wisdom as we can muster to the challenges of the office.

There is a deliberate paradox in the term 'The School of Life'. School is meant to teach us what we need to know to live; yet, as the phrase ruefully suggests, it is most often life (by which we really mean 'painful experience') that does most of the instruction for us. The real institution called The School of Life therefore carries a hope and a provocation. It dares to believe that we might learn, systematically and in good time, what we might otherwise acquire only through many decades of stumbling. And it gently criticises the current way we equip ourselves with the skills we need to thrive. We have collectively left some of what it is most important to know to chance; we have denied ourselves the opportunity to transmit wisdom, reserving our belief in education based on technical and managerial skills. The School of Life is a modest attempt to try to save us a bit of time.

20 Emotional Skills for the Workplace

1
Adaptability

For most of history, people did not believe that the world changed very much or, for that matter, that change could ever be positive. Stability and cyclicality were the ideals. The same stories were told again and again; time was understood to turn like a wheel rather than move like an arrow; technology hardly advanced; trades were handed down the generations without improvement, and the social order appeared immutable.

By contrast, we are now obsessed with, and laud, change. We are taught to regard widespread and frequent change as inescapable, and a profound advantage. We feel only pity for yesteryear and measure our virtue by our openness to continuous revolution. To confess to a fear of change is to risk being labelled as that most damned of contemporary figures: a reactionary.

Yet our adaptability to change is neither a given, nor always straightforward. The arena in which the advantages of change are at their most evident is science. The prototype helicopter built by Paul Cornu in 1907 was a gallant contraption of plywood, string and bicycle wheels. But, without dispute, it is much worse at vertical takeoff and hovering than the latest machines from AgustaWestland. The direction of change in technology is clear and the sense of progress obvious. Medicine provides countless examples of the same kind. This seduces us into supposing that change in general always brings benefits, extending a hopefulness that is justified in specific areas, such as rotor blades and antibiotics, to other areas where its relevance and legitimacy are much less secure.

Take, for example, politics and society. We know – from folklore or our own lives – that the old ways contained important truths and types of happiness that have now escaped our grasp. The villages were quieter, the shops more restricted, the manners more sober, but there was an openness to experience, a groundedness and a gratitude that we may long for in the frenzy of the kaleidoscopic present. In order to summon the will to action, to rouse ourselves and our communities from inertia, we have no choice but to tactically overestimate the advantages of change. We do this around marriage, divorce, moving country or starting a business. It's not that there will never be a great result; there will be a range of subtle losses too. Not all goods can coexist. The outcome is always more ambivalent than we can imagine. Nostalgia is not just for the simple-minded: it is a natural response to what will be lost even alongside genuine improvement.

However open to change we might be, when it comes to major upheavals we have a bad habit of being painfully unprepared. Often, they simply come too fast. For many generations, people in the ancient city of Pompeii lived a prosperous life. The soil was good; the climate kindly. They built gracious houses. They planted vineyards on the slopes of nearby Mount Vesuvius while, all along, the pressure of the magma inside slowly built up. People gave dinner parties, struggled for status, bought works of art and scanned the horizon for changes, positive and negative. No one considered the peak above the city skyline. The story of Pompeii is moving because it is a tale of innocence in which we know ourselves to be implicated at some level. For us, too, something we are blithely ignoring will be the probable cause of our sudden downfall. We are steering blind, pursuing our ordinary business on the natural assumption that whatever feels secure today will be so tomorrow. We too have no real idea where the next explosion may come from.

If we are not unprepared for sudden change, we are failing to adapt because change is so slow. The sea may be a better metaphor than a volcano. Year on year, the waves gradually eat into the rocks; complete change occurs through minute and imperceptible actions. We can't believe that small lapping motions could win against a huge edifice of rock – but they can.

Good theorists of change do not ultimately focus so much on the tempo of change; they identify fundamental features of human nature and wonder how changes will relate to them. When Thomas Edison showed off the first light bulb, it didn't seem like the world was about to be transformed. The bulb was a bizarre-looking contraption, unlike anything people would want in their homes. At first, gas was much safer and cheaper. Potential backers were sceptical. But when the great banker J.P. Morgan saw it, he grasped its possibilities at once. The bulb looked ridiculous, but only in superficial ways. Morgan saw past what was odd and off-putting and recognised an eternal idea in a strange guise. The banker was good at what we would call pattern recognition. He had the confidence and wisdom to see continuity where others thought only in terms of ugly rupture. He had seen change before, with railroads and steel, and had understood these as new approaches to age-old problems. Morgan had – as it were – studied other exploding mountains.

We underestimate opportunities for change in part because our lives are so short. We generally witness only a few revolutions directly, so we are fooled by impressions of stability, like children who consider their first home as an eternal part of the earth. Our congenital error is to imagine that what appears solid must be so. We get used to gas lamps – they have been around since we arrived on the planet – so why would they now promptly vanish? We get used to our tidy orchards maturing in the sun on the slopes of a fertile mountain, so why would an inferno come here? The error has long fascinated philosophers. Bertrand Russell imagined a turkey used to being fed by a farmer. Like us, turkeys have short memories, so when a bird hears the tread of the farmer's boots, it feels sure that it is about to be fed, as always. Then it's the week before Christmas. The turkey is a creature of habit, as we are for much of the time, but, in theory at least, we have reason and therefore a key advantage. A philosophical turkey would have wondered why the farmer was helping him every day and would have speculated about possible reasons. The presence of a mysterious factor would have haunted the imagination of the benighted animal. The response to complacency is not so much to be continually on edge as to attempt to think more deeply and more sceptically about the workings of reality.

In our responses to change, we are undermined, too, by a false sense of hierarchy about what qualifies as trivial and what is important. We carry around with us implicit and distorted ideas as to what is worth paying attention to and what we can safely ignore. The early Norwegian settlers in Greenland suffered terrible hardships, and eventually died out, because they refused to adopt the survival skills and strategies known to the Inuit inhabitants. The Norwegians could not believe that such strange-looking and apparently unsophisticated people could teach them anything. To their fatal cost, they refused to learn, because the lessons being offered came in wrappings that violated their expectations of what sophisticated intelligence could look like.

Similarly, the elite of the United Kingdom went into grave economic decline in the mid-20th century in large part because its insular characters were resistant to learning about the nature of major economic change from people they deemed their radical inferiors: rough-hewn American business folk. We reject The Beatles, or dismiss Socrates or Van Gogh as fools, because we are readier to follow a familiar script of what is valuable rather than assess the true merits of what is before us on every occasion. We forget what odd guises truly great ideas have always tended to adopt.

It is understandable why change should be so frightening or sad: we will not be around for most of it. Lingering beneath our occasional lack of adaptability is a dread of the change that will one day wipe us away. It is because we are so exposed to the inescapable reality of aging that we seek to make or protect things that will outlast us – businesses included. We have so much to cope with in terms of change in our bodies, it is no wonder that we often find ourselves interested in things that remain constant in the world outside. We start to define some of the things we most care about when we dare to ask ourselves what we hope will never change.

2
Calm

In its way, anger is a form of madness. We pick up the largest jam jar and fling it to the floor. We deliver a stream of obscenities to the attendant at the counter. We accelerate and overtake on a narrow country lane bordered by high hedges.

However illogical these moments, it is not right to dismiss them as merely beyond understanding or, for that matter, control. They operate according to an underlying rationale that can be grasped so that anger be contained and extinguished. The possibility of anger gestates around the many imperfections of existence: the internet connection has failed, the plane is delayed, someone has misunderstood a management priority. It is fair enough to take a negative view of these things. But in order for them to make us angry – rather than merely sad – something else needs to be at work psychologically: hope. We break, kick, slam and accelerate because we are, at some level, horribly optimistic.

Although the angry may seem negatively predisposed to life, they are in their hearts recklessly hopeful. How badly we react to frustration is critically determined by what we think of as normal. We may be irritated that it is raining, but our pessimistic accommodation to the likelihood of showers means we are unlikely to respond to one by screaming. Our annoyance is tempered by what we understand we can expect from the climate; by our melancholy experience of what is normal to hope for from the skies. We aren't overwhelmed by anger whenever we don't get something we want, only when we first believed ourselves entitled to secure it and then did not. Our greatest furies spring from events that violate our sense of the ground rules of existence.

The intemperately wrathful operate with the wrong sense of what is normal. The person who shouts every time they lose their house keys betrays a faith – touching, were it not so damaging – that their belongings should never go astray. The person who loses their temper when stuck behind a slow driver evinces a curious (and potentially murderous) belief that country roads should always be traffic-free.

Any move towards greater calm therefore has to begin with pessimism. We must learn to disappoint ourselves at leisure before the world has a chance to slap us by surprise, when our defences are down. The angry must be systematically inducted to the darkest realities of life, to the stupidities of others, to the ineluctable failings of technology, to the necessary flaws of infrastructure, while there is still a relative measure of rational control. They should start each day with a short but thorough meditation on the many humiliations and insults they might be subjected to in the coming hours, from a car crash to the accidental destruction of their livelihoods.

One way to foster calm was worked out by the ancient Roman philosophers of the Stoic school. These Stoics proposed that we should see ourselves as always hovering between a free and a determined state; able to control certain things, but at the mercy of events in other areas. They invented a powerful image to evoke our condition as creatures sometimes able to effect great change, yet never far from being subject to powerful external necessities. We are, they said, like dogs who have been tied to an unpredictable cart. Our leash is long enough to give us a degree of leeway, but not long

_____ We may be powerless to alter certain events, but we remain free to choose our attitude towards them.

enough to allow us to wander wherever we please. A dog will naturally hope to go wherever it pleases, said the Stoics. But if it cannot, it is better for the animal to be trotting behind the cart than dragged and strangled by it.

To reflect that we too are never without a leash around our neck may help to reduce the violence of our protest against events that veer away from our intentions. This may sound like a recipe for passivity, but, as the Stoics insisted, it is no less unreasonable to accept something as necessary when it isn't as to rebel against something when it is.

We must use reason to judge the difference, and this is where we have a big advantage over a dog. A dog will probably not at first grasp that he is even tied to a cart, nor understand the connection between the swerves of the cart and the pain in his neck. So he won't be able to predict where the cart is going and adjust his position accordingly. But reason enables us to theorise with considerable accuracy about the path of the cart (or destiny). This offers us a chance – unique among living beings – to increase our sense of freedom by ensuring a good slack between our desires and what we cannot change. Reason allows us to calculate when our wishes are in irrevocable conflict with reality, and then bids us to submit ourselves willingly, rather than angrily or bitterly, to necessities. We may be powerless to alter certain events, but we remain free to choose our attitude towards them. It is in an unprotesting acceptance of what is truly necessary that we can find serenity and freedom.

The angry are also scared. They may seem bullishly

confident in their rage, but they smash things up out of panic. They have no faith in their own capacity to survive frustration and recover equanimity despite some perhaps truly significant losses. They lack a resilient sense of how error and damage may be repaired, borne and overcome with sufficient patience, love and time.

Behind their outbursts, the angry are trying to teach the world things: how to run an airline, how to drive, how to make decent conversation with a client. However, they are exceptionally bad teachers because too much is at stake for them. We tend to laugh at the angry (when we are not terrified of their blows), but when we can manage it, we should bear in mind that their anger is grounded in attitudes and hopes that may deserve sympathy rather than scorn. The bulging eyes, the raised voices and the harsh phrases occur when an intense sense of justice and urgent practical energy meet the conviction that they will not be understood or listened to if they try to explain their disappointments. Given what has caused the outburst in the first place, to calm down the angry person tends only to require three things: a ready declaration that we too are extremely disappointed, a sympathetic insistence that we wish it could be otherwise, and a magnanimous and convincingly delivered assurance that we are sure they will get through this.

3
Charm

Persuasiveness and idealisation

The art of persuading someone to buy something lies at the heart of business. However, we often internalise images of selling drawn from capitalism's worst moments, which gives those involved in the persuasion game an unhelpful background sense of shame. But the moral status of salesmanship isn't fixed: everything depends on the value of what is being sold, and the manner in which it is being advanced. Good persuasion means the art of honestly uniting an audience with the elements it requires to flourish to its full potential.

A central reason why salesmanship goes wrong is due to a feeling that the only way to prove acceptable to a buyer is through exaggeration; through a perverse perfectionism projected onto the imagined audience.

The Netherlands Board of Tourism is responsible for marketing the Dutch countryside. To lure visitors, it employs images of neat windmills bordering pristine canals, with bright flowers along the banks and permanently sunny skies. There are some places that on one or two days of the year – particularly near Leiden in late July – the Netherlands looks exactly like this. But there are many other, more typical, aspects of the Dutch countryside that the Board of Tourism stays quiet about: it's almost always overcast; there are many places where there's not a flower to be seen; it rains most days; and there's always a lot of mud. You will encounter many a wonky old sluice gate and some rickety palings shoring up the banks.

A captivating – but not
necessarily realistic – image
designed to attract visitors to
the Netherlands.

Selling the Netherlands
in a more 'honest' way,
sullen clouds and incipient
rain included.
__Jacob van Ruisdael,
The Windmill at Wijk
bij Duurstede, 1670.

In order to avoid an awkward collision with reality, the Board of Tourism would have been wise to consult a painting in the nation's main art gallery, the Rijksmuseum, by the 17th-century artist Jacob van Ruisdael. Van Ruisdael loved the Dutch countryside; he spent as much time there as he could, and he was keen to let everyone know what he liked about it. But instead of selecting a special (and unrepresentative) spot and waiting for a rare and fleeting moment of bright sunshine, he adopted a very different 'selling' strategy.

Van Ruisdael's most famous painting is an advert for the qualities he discovered. He loved overcast days and carefully studied the fascinating movements of stormy skies. He was entranced by the infinite gradations of grey and how you'll often see a patch of fluffy white brightness drifting behind a darker, billowing mass of rain-dense clouds. He did not deny that there was mud or that the river and canal banks are frequently messy. Instead, he noticed their special kind of beauty and made a case for it.

The Netherlands Board of Tourism, like so many corporations, felt that the reality of what it was selling was unacceptable and so resorted – for the nicest reasons, and out of a touching modesty – to lies. But the real Dutch countryside has many merits: it is quiet and solemn; it encourages tranquil contemplation; it offers an antidote to stress and forced cheerfulness. These are things we might really need to help us cope with our overloaded and often inauthentic lives.

In all acts of successful selling, what matters is an honest foregrounding of a thing's actual virtues, and a confidence that these will prove enough.

It is not easy to sell this way, because it requires an all-too-elusive confidence to sidestep the standard over-bright approaches. But it is a confidence that should emerge from an understanding of a basic fact of human psychology: we are prepared to accept the less than perfect if we can be guided to appreciate it with skill, confidence and charm. Exaggeration is only a nervous first move in salesmanship. But, as we know (yet keep forgetting), things sell best over the long term when their real, albeit modest, merits have been intelligently brought out.

Like van Ruisdael, a series of adverts used by Volkswagen in the 1960s explored the appeal of the ordinary and the allure of candour. These unusually modest adverts became classics of marketing in a more 'authentic' way. Like a charming, mature person, the adverts were able to admit that their product was not perfect. VW had the confidence of experience, which teaches us that no one's life is more than a distant shot at perfection. The job is far from flawless, but it's still a decent place to work. The children's school has some major drawbacks, but it does some things very well. Our partner is all too human, as are we. The approach VW uses is beguiling because it addresses us as the adults we really are; it trusts us with the truth about the world.

Unfortunately, advertising agencies have forgotten these lessons and grown infatuated with exaggeration. This has grave repercussions for the appeal of their advertising.

They are no longer a true friend of what they are selling – a friend being someone who likes you not because they fail to notice

Volkswagen campaign,
1964.

And if you run out of gas, it's easy to push.

See?
We think of everything.
Getting a Volkswagen to the side of the road is a pushover.
It's a little surprising that VW owners don't run out of gas more often.
A figure like 32 miles to the gallon can make you a little hazy about when you

last filled up.
And you spend so little time in gas stations, there are almost no reminders.
You'll probably never need oil between changes, for example.
You'll never need water or anti-freeze because the engine is air-cooled.
40,000 miles on a set of tires won't break

any Volkswagen records.
And repairs are few and far between.
So this year we've installed a gas gauge to help you remember.
But we haven't taken all the fun away.
You still have to remember to look at it.

the ways in which you are less than ideal, but because they appreciate your merits and sympathise with your tribulations and weaknesses nevertheless. The best kind of salesmanship helps us recognise, and properly esteem, the worth of the life almost all of us are required to live: an ordinary one.

Shouting and persuading

At breakfast, you are confronted by a smallish portable billboard, which also doubles as a container for cereal.

There is quite a lot that the box wants to communicate, with the goal of getting us to buy further packets next time we're at the supermarket. Over breakfast we learn that the cereal will charge into our lives like a train hurtling towards us across wheat fields; that the product is bursting with fibre; that it's filled with sunlight and blue skies and made from perfect ears of corn. And don't forget its nutritional advantages, either.

But the box is worried. It's anxious that we might not be paying attention. It imagines that the ambient noise at this moment is quite loud. Maybe we're listening to news of a political scandal; glancing at the weather forecast; coordinating the day with our partner; or trying to think where a child's boots could be hiding.

With all this competition around, the cereal box wants to cut through and make us listen to what it has to say. To do this, it shouts. It uses the strongest colour contrasts and ramps up the intensity: the sky intensely blue, the wheat perfectly golden, the lettering huge – the box makes point-blank assertions about the virtues of its content.

A typical breakfast cereal box tends to 'shout' the message of its virtues.

Every bit of the surface has been used to keep the volume as high as possible. If it could, it might fit flashing lights and a claxon.

But there are other ways in which messages get across and win our attention in a crowded world. Shouting is not the only option, it's just a very familiar one at the moment. An alternative was explored by the English artist Ben Nicholson.

From the mid-1930s, Nicholson specialised in low-key, semi-abstract works, in which different shades of white were juxtaposed and laid on top of one another, rendering us acutely conscious of the variations in tone between whites. His work was very quiet indeed. Nicholson was seeking to dim the volume of what he was saying to the extent that others would have to turn down the ambient noise and focus.

Nicholson realised that, for all that's going on around us, we remain highly responsive to certain dim signals. Something can stand out from the crowd precisely because it is quiet. This is a quality we recognise and like in some people – in those who don't have to raise their voices to be listened to and who can hold the attention of a room even though they speak without assertion and pause between sentences. Shouting may get attention; it rarely persuades.

Too often, selling has become confused with pestering. Advertising annoys; it turns up at awkward times and in places where it's not wanted. It spoils the street, the side of the bus and the introduction to the film. But the problem isn't selling as such; it's trying to sell to the wrong person at the wrong time.

Badgering has two characteristics: randomness and

This all-white artwork offers
a quiet refuge from an
exhaustingly noisy world.
__Ben Nicholson, *1935 (white
relief)*.

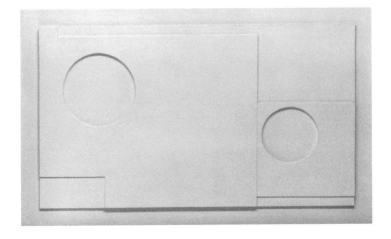

untimeliness. In relationships, badgering becomes nagging. Here the aim might be reasonable – this person should take out the rubbish or clean the bathroom. But the approach is held back by simple repetition of the demand at inopportune moments and a lack of insight into what is holding the person back from doing what you want. Nagging ends up making compliance less likely. At its most extreme in love, badgering gives us the stalker. It's the person who knows they are keen on someone but has no view of why the other would be interested in them. They have no seductive resources, they just impose themselves in an unpleasant manner.

There is a commercial version of this that buys a little acquiescence in the short term but loses goodwill on the whole. Badgering grows from an unflattering and mistaken picture of the customer. It supposes someone who can only respond to loud noises; who can only be won over by repetition; who can only respond to vulgar signals. This isn't how the sellers themselves feel and behave, but they don't think of their audience as being like them in this regard. They lose touch with their own experience when devising their selling strategy.

Badgering and nagging have a history in our own lives. We used these strategies as babies, when we had no other options. We resorted to them when we were six and had no capacity to rationally persuade our parents to buy us a goldfish but instinctively assumed that asking a million times would work (occasionally it does). This is where we all have come from. We carry a lot of residue. And when we're under pressure, we return to these early instincts.

The path of growth towards adulthood, and therefore good salesmanship, involves getting better at understanding the needs of those we are addressing. The badgering child can't understand why the parent won't agree or what their values really are. The child thinks maybe they've forgotten the demand (in the last three minutes) and that they should therefore ask again. Good growth means becoming more aware of what the parent's reservations might be.

The art of persuasion evolves through working out how to address real concerns. At fourteen, the child might be drawing up a little document called: 'Why I should be allowed to go on the school trip to Berlin'. Growth also involves becoming more sensitive to context. The child might learn that their aunt's rather luxurious flat is not a good place to ask their parents for anything, because that place make them feel anxious about money. They know that their mother is likely to listen carefully at 3pm on Sunday, and not at all at 7.45am on Monday. Or that the drive home from school is the ideal time to make a big request.

What is needed all around is greater trust. Trust arises when the seller is seeking to make a profit from making a valuable contribution to the customer's life. We only become friends with people we can trust. To date, that hasn't encompassed the advertising industry, from whose advances we keep fleeing, so often have we been pestered – even though we need and want to buy things on a regular basis. Persuaders need to behave with the sort of dignity and self-respect of people who know they could properly improve the lives of customers. Along the way, they might learn to speak in quieter voices.

_____ A good life is not one immune to grief, but one in which we allow suffering to contribute to our development.

Cheeriness

Across history, the articulation of gloomy attitudes in works of art has provided us with relief from a sense of loneliness and persecution. Among others, Pascal, Keats, Shelley, Schopenhauer and Leonard Cohen have been able to reassure us of the normality of our states of sadness. In particular, they have made a case for melancholy; a species of low-level, muted sadness that arises when we are open to the fact that life is inherently difficult and that suffering and disappointment are core parts of universal experience. It is not a disorder that needs to be cured. The good life is not one immune to grief, but one in which we allow suffering to contribute to our development.

Yet the dominant tone of salesmanship continues to be cheerful, or its more brittle cousin, cheery – a good mood that tolerates no other. There have only ever been a handful of melancholy adverts. This presumes that the best way to please others is to present ourselves in a vibrant mood. But the central move of melancholy art is to help us by not trying to cheer us up. It doesn't attempt to suggest that it doesn't matter that a parent has died, that one has been sacked or that a novel one has been working on for seven years has been rejected.

The idea that kindness lies in not trying to cheer us up was at the heart of the work of Charles Baudelaire. The French poet was well acquainted with grief. He had a miserable relationship with his socially prominent stepfather; he was addicted to gambling; he was infected with syphilis at an early age; he squandered his inheritance. He found the process of writing agonising. In the opening of his collection, *Les Fleurs du Mal*, he addresses the reader directly:

— Hypocrite lecteur, — mon semblable, — mon frère!
[you — hypocrite reader — my double — my brother!]

Baudelaire was not out to insult us; he was acknowledging that we often pretend to be happier than we really are, but indicated that his own poems would not make such demands upon us. He was offering a kind of companionship based on knowing troubles from the inside. He was taking the leap of presuming to know the scale of our inner confusion.

Advertisers could usefully extend their emotional range; to learn to meet us in other moods, because there are so many needs we are more alive to when we acknowledge our sadness. We don't stop being consumers when we're down, but we have different priorities. Admission of our despair, and the number of moments when we wonder if it can really be worth it, are key tools in the process of selling properly reimagined.

The good seller remembers how much of life deserves solemn and mournful states, and how much loyalty we might be ready to offer those who don't feel aggressively compelled to deny our melancholy.

4
Communication

The challenges

We have done so much to overcome the more obvious, external barriers to communication. We have ringed the earth with satellites and enlaced it with cables. At a surface level, we are always available. But ironically, the trickiest obstacles to communication continue to occur in what seem like the most favourable circumstances: when we're standing in a room close to another person who speaks, ostensibly, exactly our language.

To be a good communicator at a psychological level, we need to be equipped with the very best kind of emotional education. We need an ability to understand what we ourselves think and feel; confidence that we will be able to make ourselves heard by others; the capacity to be patient and non-aggressive in relaying messages; the skill to evade the defence mechanisms or boredom of our listeners; an open-mindedness in hearing ideas that could sound foreign or threatening; and, finally, a culture that lends legitimacy to the idea of people talking frankly to one another about the most vital things.

Despite our extraordinary prowess at the technical side of communication, humans have made very little progress towards improving the quality of psychological communication between ourselves. We still too often fall into sulks and furies; we don't say what is on our minds or fail to get our points across. Despite all the masts and satellites, there are still too many children not communicating honestly with their parents, couples not listening to each other and colleagues not finding the right words. There are still too many suicide notes and deathbeds on which the majority is left unsaid. So much of what we want to say remains locked up inside us, or travels between humans as unreliably as the pigeon post of two hundred years ago.

The remarkable need to speak

It sounds absurd when stated baldly, but we do not always understand that we need to speak to those whom we so wish would understand us. We long for our intentions to be known, for our moods to be honoured, for our states of mind to be read – but we do not want to speak and we don't particularly see an urgent need to do so. We want to be guessed at, intuited, read by a kind of magic we don't realise we believe in. We want people to know what we have not bothered to tell them. In certain moods, we may even suspect that they know full well what we think and want, but are deliberately frustrating us in order to score points and humiliate us. The only explanations for them not having guessed already is rudeness, lack of love or extreme stupidity.

We think like this not because we are evil: we are stubbornly mute because we were, for a short but profound length of time, infants. In other words, for a momentous stretch, we were in the odd position where we could not utter a word. Others had to guess what was on our minds. And most importantly, for a while, they were more or less correct. They listened to our crying, witnessed our angry faces, saw our outstretched arms... they had a shot at guessing and they got it right. They fetched some milk; they picked up our toy from the floor; they put us on their shoulder and walked us around the living room – and we felt calm and satiated. They were not geniuses at interpersonal understanding: they guessed correctly because it was easy. The things we needed back then were so uncomplicated and so limited: food and drink, clean clothes, sleep, hygiene and reassurance.

This ancestral memory of successful mind-reading has the paradoxical effect of making us more isolated and intemperate than we need to be in later life. We keep expecting that a process that unfolded successfully when we were young might continue to occur – even though our needs have grown infinitely more sophisticated. We don't just need milk and a cuddle: we need people to understand how our diary is looking next week; what the hand we put around them in bed means; how the kitchen should be left; where the towels need to hang; how the document should get back to the NY office; who should have the remote control; and how we feel about their mother.

And we want them to know all this not on the basis of careful and slow instructions and eloquent, patient and playful disquisitions, but immediately, just like that, on the basis that they are intelligent and that they care for us. If they don't understand, there might be cause to shout, to accuse them of laziness or a lack of affection or to fire them.

We are terrible communicators because we refuse to accept the dignity, necessity and complexity of the act of communication. We wander the earth with the problems of sophisticated adults insisting on believing that we are as easy to understand as infants.

On suffering in silence

Despite a lot of encouragement, despite political freedoms and psychological exhortations, most of us still suffer in silence. We don't say – until it is far too late – what is wrong, what we want, how we are angry, what we're ashamed of and the way we would like things to be.

Perhaps it shouldn't be a surprise how hard speaking up continues to feel. For most of the history of humanity, speaking up was about the most dangerous thing an ordinary human could do. There were mighty superiors above us who demanded complete obedience and were strictly uninterested in anything we might have to say. Speaking up would have got us flogged, excommunicated or killed. Democracy is, at best, some two hundred and fifty years old, and our psychological development has a habit of lagging far beyond our social realities. Long after a war is over, we respond with the fears of the hunted. Centuries after the last feudal lord moved into an apartment in town, we behave with some of the meek humility of the cowed serf.

In personal life, similar principles of submission have applied. Throughout history, a good child did not speak up. If we were sad, we cried softly into our pillow at night. If we mistakenly spilt some ink, we tried to hide the evidence. The adult does not have to be an outright bully to disable a child. If they are often on edge, preoccupied by matters at work, seem depressed and close to breakdown, or have elevated yet rigid ideals of who their offspring should be, the child might as well have a belt around their mouth.

For most of the years human beings have been on

this planet, we have had a history of festering, sulking, bitterness, suppressed rage, bitten lips and of saying nothing openly. Only very recently – in the last second, from an evolutionary perspective – have we woken to the possible benefits and occasional necessity of speaking up.

In an office, we know that it is good if people lower down the organisation speak up to those towards the top. We know that it is good, in love, if partners who feel aggrieved and sad about something (however small and petty it might sound) speak up, so as to be able to feel affection and desire once more. We know in families that it is good if children manage to tell their parents they're not interested in certain sorts of jobs or complain if they are being mistreated.

But the legacies of our unfreedom abound. We smile a little too readily; we try a little too hard to appease; we are a little too slow to articulate a hurt. In this respect, we aren't being nice: we are just scared and ashamed. Our friendliness is born not out of choice, but out of an inability to dare to cause upset.

To learn to speak up requires two rather odd-sounding things. First is a recognition that, at some level, we are afraid that we will be killed if we speak. It sounds odd and humiliating, but that is how little children feel when Dad has slammed the door or Mum has said enough times, 'You'll be the end of me'. A vital part of our picture of what will happen if we speak has been formed in our childhood imagination. Secondly, we need to acknowledge the adult truth that we will not be killed, because enough people have already died on our behalf to guarantee us freedom of speech (as well as our right to cross town and start a new life somewhere else). We need to turn what is enshrined in law into what finally feels believable to us psychologically – and, bravely, speak up.

Impatient teaching; resentful learning

We are irritated and upset by the fact that people don't understand or grasp crucial things that we need them to know. More particularly, and paradoxically, we are furious at them for not knowing something that we assume they should know without ever having been taught. And we have not taught them what we are convinced they must know for a fundamental reason: we don't respect teaching very much.

We respect teachers in theory and we pay lip service to the concept of education, but in practice, teaching may feel like a dull and unworthy occupation. It bored us for years at school and now we tend to be happy to leave it to other, lesser, mortals. Yet teaching is one of the most central, unavoidable and in many ways noble aspects of communal life. Even if we haven't signed up to instruct adolescents in maths or languages, even if we aren't interested in telling someone how to find the area of a circle or ask for a train ticket in French, we are called upon to 'teach' almost every hour of every day. We need to teach others how we're feeling, what we want, what is paining us, the way we think things should be. The teaching specialisation we have to take on is a bizarre-sounding but crucial subject: *Who I Am and What I Care About*. Yet in many areas, we rush over the curriculum and skip to the punishment phase. We fail to get others to see what matters so much to us: why we were hurt by that sarcastic remark over dinner;

_____ Teaching is a basic psychological manoeuvre upon which the health of every community, relationship and office depends.

why we are maddened when people speak out of turn at a meeting; why it wouldn't be a good idea to pull together a committee to explore the proposal. We have fatally misconstrued teaching as a specific professional job, when really it is a basic psychological manoeuvre upon which the health of every community, relationship and office depends.

'Teaching' is the infinitely complex art of getting an idea, insight, emotion or skill from one human brain into another. Whatever the subject matter, the core requirements for this tend to be the same. The first and foremost is that the person we are teaching should not be scared, angry or hurt. We cannot learn when we have been humiliated or belittled, insulted or threatened. Few of us can take ideas on board when we have been called fools and idiots. Our minds are not at their most receptive until we have been patiently comforted, reassured of our value and given licence to fail.

The second core related requirement is that the teacher not panic. A hysterical teacher has already lost the capacity to accomplish their goals. It is a paradox that our teaching efforts are more likely to succeed the less manically we care that they will come off. Being in a position not to mind too much if our lessons haven't really had the desired impact can be the best way of ensuring that we will stay patient with the student – and thereby succeed. A sense that everything is at stake and the world is ending – easy enough impressions to reach in relationships or at work – guarantees to turn us into catastrophic pedagogues.

The good teacher also knows that timing is critical to successful instruction. We tend automatically to try to teach a lesson the moment the problem arises, rather than when it is most likely to be attended to (which might be several days later). We typically end up addressing the most delicate and complex teaching tasks just when we feel most scared and distressed and our 'student' is most exhausted and nervous. We should learn to proceed like a wily general who knows how to wait for just the right conditions to make a move. We should develop a cult of great timing in addressing tricky matters, passing down stories from generation to generation of how, after years of getting nowhere with impulse-driven frontal assaults, a great teacher stood patiently by the dishwasher until their partner had put down the newspaper, then carefully advanced a long-prepared point, and eventually won a decisive victory.

When we give up on teaching (and therefore, on those we need to teach), we tend to manoeuvre around the objects of our despair. We tell them their work is fine, but silently redo it with other colleagues. We set up secret side groups. It is meant to be a collaboration between twenty equals, but we go out and hire two external consultants. It might sound Machiavellian, but it's merely the outcome of a nervous personality with low faith in others and in the chances of working through problems. Secret manoeuvring is a vote of no confidence in the possibilities of persuasion or education. It is the result of a big conclusion somewhere in the mind: that nothing good can come of dealing with people directly.

It isn't always easy to be the student either. To accept that one needs to learn requires a tolerance of one's own ignorance, and therefore of the vulnerability that comes from not yet being in complete command of an important area. There can be a temptation to bluster that one is already on top of the brief or else to insist that something isn't worth learning to begin with; these are the defensive paths of bullshit or denigration.

The defensive have no trust in the benevolence of teachers. In their minds, there is no distinction between a comment on their work and a criticism of their right to exist. Defensiveness raises the cost of disagreement – and thereby dialogue – intolerably.

Somewhere in the early past of the defensive person, there would have been a sense of grave danger about being in the subordinate, as-yet-unfinished position, which inspired a flight into precocious hypercompetence. What now seems impressive masks brittleness and fear of collapse.

It is the task of all parents to break bad news to their offspring. But there are rather different ways of going about the challenge. The best sort of pedagogy leaves the child at once aware of a need to improve and with a sense of being liked despite their ignorance and flaws. Yet there are also cases where criticism cuts too deep, where the child is left not just corrected but tarred with an impression of worthlessness. To recognise without shame and to understand sympathetically why one has become defensive is the key to unwinding the habits of excessive self-protection and therefore of opening oneself up to education and improvement. We needed those defences once; now we can afford to let them go. Knowing how to learn and grow means having a capacity to forgive oneself for one's incompetence – and the (very predictable) horrors of the first draft.

Nagging

When teaching and learning fail, we enter the realm of nagging. Nagging is the dispiriting, unpleasant, counter-productive but wholly understandable and poignant version of a hugely noble ambition: the desire for change.

There is so much we might fairly want to change about people. We want them to be more self-aware, punctual, generous, reliable, introspective, resilient, communicative, profound... At home, we want them to focus more on the sink, the children, the bins, the money and the need to put the phone down and look up. At a macro dimension, we want them to think more about the suffering of encaged animals, the destruction of our habitat and the iniquities of capitalism. The desire to change people is no pathology; it is a clear-sighted recognition of the scale of human wickedness.

Nagging is, in its essence, a version of teaching that has given up hope. It has descended into an attempt to insist rather than invite, to coerce rather than charm. We have grown too weary and humiliated by constant rebuffs to have the energy to seduce. We are too panicked by the thought that the unteachable 'student' is ruining our life to find the inner resources to see it more from their point of view. Our own suffering dominates all the available imaginative capacity.

And so, we get straight to the point, get rid of the garlands, omit the honey and say things in plain terms. The bins need attention now. Get to the table immediately. You're a selfish layabout. Not there, here... We aren't wrong. We are very right, but also very tired and, deep down, grief-stricken.

_____ As soon as a student starts to feel humiliated, the lesson is over.

Lamentably, nagging doesn't actually work. As soon as a student starts to feel humiliated, the lesson is over. Nagging breeds its evil twin: shirking. They pretend to read the paper, go upstairs and feel righteous. The shrillness of our tone gives them all the excuse they need to trust that we have nothing kind or true to tell them.

We can change others only when the desire that they evolve has not reached an insistent pitch, when we can still bear that they remain as they are. We improve only when we have not been made to feel guilty; only when we have a sense that we are loved and understood for the many reasons why change is so hard for us. We know, of course, that the bins need our attention, that we should strive to get to bed earlier and that we have been a disappointment. But we can't bear to hear these lessons in an unsympathetic tone. Tricky children that we are, we want to be indulged for our ambivalence about becoming better people.

The same obtuse dynamic is at play at the political level. We know we shouldn't abuse the planet, bend rules or close our hearts to the unfortunate. But we won't do any of the good things if a dour figure wags their finger and delivers stern lectures. We want to be charmed, not dragged, into goodness.

The tragedy of nagging is that the intentions behind it are usually so noble, and yet it doesn't work. We nag because we feel that our possession of the truth lets us off having to convey it elegantly. It never does. The solution to nagging is not to give up trying to get others to do what we want; it is to recognise that persuasion needs to occur in terms that make sense to those we want to alter.

5
Confidence

One reason why our confidence fails is that we become anxious about losing our dignity. Many situations that could be interesting and enjoyable also carry a palpable danger of making fools of us. If we try to strike up a conversation with someone, it could be the start of something great, but the risk is that they'll turn away and think we're idiots for presuming that they might be interested. If we go on our own to a party where we don't really know anyone, we could end up having an interesting evening, but it's also possible that we'll look out of place and pitifully lonely. We could ask frankly for a raise or a promotion, but some senior person might view our request as a sign that we've badly misjudged our merit. When we say we lack confidence, what we often really mean is that we regularly give up on an alluring but uncertain opportunity so as to avoid a possible blow to our pride.

Our fear stems from the touching idea that we need to protect our dignity in order to live well. Our mental picture of ourselves is that we're not idiots, and therefore it would be terrible if others thought that we were. But the strangely helpful fact is that we are definitely fools already. Not because there's anything particularly strange about us as individuals: this is just a basic truth about being alive. Of course we're driven by irrational impulses; of course we want things we won't get; obviously we'll make remarks that we'll later regret; we will inevitably misread situations and make others think we're a touch bizarre. This is what happens on a regular basis if you have a human brain, wander the world and interact with other people. For the underconfident person, the way to lower anxiety is to admit that we are fools already and therefore have little to lose. The worst that can happen is that others recognise what we already acknowledge as true. We won't be affronted by an attack on our self-conception, we'll merely have confirmation of what we know from the outset. And, if we do take the risk, sometimes things will go pleasingly in our favour: we'll get the occasional kiss; we'll make a new friend; our request will be met with a warm smile.

Another major way in which a lack of confidence shows up is when it strikes us that we are impostors. We have somehow ended up in a position around others who are much more competent and together than we are. For now they seem to believe in us, but the day must surely come when they see through us. They will recognise how ignorant and incapable and clumsy we really are, and we will be brusquely rejected.

Impostor syndrome builds on our natural reluctance to extend what we know of ourselves to others. We know from the inside all the things that are wrong with us. But we have only a highly edited and limited picture of the reality of others. This is a structural imbalance that becomes massively developed in childhood. It is more or less unavoidable. To a young child, a parent is a god-like creature, endowed with incredible levels of intelligence and power. They can drive a car and lift us up almost to the ceiling; they could do our maths homework in two seconds. And these impressive qualities are wrapped up in an alien nature. It feels as if the grown-ups are not like us at all: they don't like wriggling under the sofa; they go to meetings; they talk for ages with their friends.

_____ The people we are so impressed by are much more like us than we think.

This way of seeing the world becomes so familiar that we keep on imagining that we are encountering new versions of it, for example when we move to a job we feel lucky to get or start a high-powered university course.

When we were little, it was impossible for us to recognise that the adults around us were muddled, insecure and far from fully mature. The same goes for when we feel like impostors. The people we are so impressed by are much more like us than we think. We can't see the details, but they are there. There are quirks and sorrows and worries and failings that loom large in their lives but that we don't directly know. We see the reasonable, skilled surface. We don't know the resignation letter they think of writing but haven't yet, or the aching fear that they are wasting their lives, the troubles at home or the mistakes they made at many points. But we can be sure that there are many things of this nature in their lives, because they are in the lives of everyone. They too are fools, for the same underlying reason we are. Almost certainly, some of the people we are most impressed by know all about impostor syndrome, because they feel it themselves. If we could go to the session in which the CEO is being mentored by a retired ex-board member we would be shocked, then relieved, by the inner doubts and worries they would express: how they are terrified they are not up to the job, how everyone looks to them and they don't know what they really think, and how nervous they felt before making a presentation to the shareholders.

The fear of being an impostor is resolved not when we become sure of our abilities but when we recognise that we are not unusual in doubting ourselves. It's not that we stop being impostors, but that we realise that everyone else is too, and that our normal quota of self-doubt has very little to do with the actual contribution that any of us can make.

6
Creativity

'Creativity' is one of the most highly praised and prestigious concepts in modern business. A large and lucrative market has emerged, feeding off some ill-focused insecurities. At worst, in a bid to increase creativity, senior executives may be sent to do finger painting or are let loose on a dressing-up box.

But business creativity is different from artistic creativity. A company is a group of individuals gathered together to solve a problem for other people. This helps to define what the true focus of business creativity should be: intense and lateral thinking about what could be missing from customers' lives. Business creativity involves skill at identifying and profitably meeting the needs (many of them unspoken and vague) of an audience. Everything else – the factories, the technology, the logistics, the spreadsheets – is secondary to this aim. Whatever efforts are subsequently lavished on execution, a business cannot succeed if it hasn't zeroed in on a real, sufficiently urgent, human requirement.

A good business understands our needs better than any competitor. Therefore, the creativity that really counts – and that companies should attempt to foster – is the one that best helps a business to enter the minds of its customers accurately and powerfully.

The stresses of running any business with even moderate success are all-consuming. It is no wonder, therefore, that enterprises sometimes lack the time to stand back and think creatively – and suffer accordingly. Nevertheless, we can get into the habit of mentally 'standing back' and wondering whether the future of our business could be a bit different, and richer, than its past.

We can start by wondering what customers might secretly be hoping for. It sounds odd, but many customers privately harbour hopes of companies that go a long way beyond what is currently on offer.

Take some of the feelings that hover around financial services. When we step back, a bank is not just a place to store money safely, with a competitive interest rate and decent customer service. We want these things, of course, but the less articulated secret hope is about something else: help in living well around money.

We have questions about how to deal with envy, worries about what to spend money on, speculations about how to build up capital and a desire to teach children about the value of money. There are big opportunities for the financial sector in better understanding people's biggest needs and ambitions around their income. A wide path to growth emerges whenever companies see themselves as being able to tackle not just a local issue but one of the big themes of existence.

It is easy for a company to become fixated on the medium in which it first launched and therefore to fail to see that its helpful moves could happily and lucratively transfer. Of any current business activity we can ask ourselves: what is the bigger version? What is the underlying principle within the business? What would it look like for the business to apply the principle in larger ways?

When teasing out the underlying principle of a business, we shouldn't look at what the company actually does so much as the move it is making. The principle of a nut manufacturer isn't packaging nuts; it is making healthy snacks. The principle of a phone company isn't making phones; it is communication. This means that one can imagine the business operating in ways that remain faithful to its principles yet involve quite different products and services.

The underlying principle of the paper clip company is temporary order. The paper clip is a beautifully simple micro-tool devoted to keeping sheaves of paper in order, while allowing them to be easily released. It was an advance on binding (which also orders papers but in a more permanent fashion, at odds with the need to extract particular sheets). The larger version of this activity could lie in filing cabinets, shelving, bags and briefcases – in each case, the same principle is involved. One day, the paper clip company could logically get around to car parks.

Or take a company that is currently making ear plugs. Its underlying principle is quiet. It taps into the need for serenity, for focus in a noisy world, where sound is a disturbing and intrusive factor. This could lead it into a range of new markets: noise-cancelling equipment, acoustic insulation or scented candles that promote tranquillity. They might develop a brand of fee-paying luxury restrooms that are havens of quiet, or reinvent the monastery as a secular retreat.

The products that any company currently offers tend to be only a small part of the customer's real needs in a given area. Creatively redefining the business area that a company is working in radically alters the sense of what its core tasks might be – and therefore where its richest future opportunities might lie.

7
Decisiveness

Indecision spoils everything, but it is originally provoked by a belief that there is an error-free way of doing things, and that it might be possible never to spoil anything.

Often mistaken for laziness, procrastination is really a species of terror, founded on a fear of the possible consequences of messing up. The best way to address the disease is therefore to reduce the imagined spectre of failure, and to gently raise the spectre of inaction, which is never cost-free. We get down to work when the fear of doing nothing at all finally exceeds the fear of doing something badly.

The indecisive person is a perfectionist. Perfectionism is the unreasonable and self-defeating ambition of getting something absolutely right, which makes us difficult to be around and punishing to live with. The origins of perfectionism lie in the imagination – in the ease with which we can conjure up a picture of an ideal state of affairs, compared with the monstrous difficulty of bringing such a state into being by ourselves. The sickness of perfectionism gestates in the fertile gap between our noble visions and our mediocre reality.

And yet, our problems do not ultimately arise in our love of perfection per se. They lie in our reckless tendencies to under-budget for the difficulties of achieving it. The proper target for (gentle) criticism is premature perfectionism. How accurately we predict the time and effort involved in a task depends on a proper grasp of its inherent difficulty. If we fully recognise something to be exceptionally arduous, we don't panic when our first efforts are weak and our progress slow. The task is difficult, but we knew it would be. High standards only become a problem when we think something might and should be substantially easier than it turns out, and when we read our struggles as marks of our own ineptitude rather than as an inevitable part of a legitimately lengthy journey.

Perfectionism is only a problem because we have inaccurately anticipated the level of difficulty, not because we are aiming high. It strikes when we imagine we might write a good novel in six months, or have a good career by the age of thirty, or have spontaneously worked out how to have a successful marriage.

Our perfectionism starts to torture us when we lack information on how hard others had to work and how much they had to suffer before reaching their ideas of perfection. In an ideal world, our culture would endlessly draw our attention to the first drafts and hidden labours of others, and properly alert us to the horrors exacted by anything worth doing. We would not then be impatient and sickly perfectionists; we would be resilient questers for excellence. The problem is not that we're aiming for perfection; it's that we don't have an accurately redemptive idea of what perfection really demands.

We are frequently thrown into anxious indecision by our need to make a choice between options, in situations where we lack the necessary information and cannot be certain of the future. We are in a state of existential angst. At such moments, it pays to remember that the real choice is almost never between error and happiness, but between varieties of suffering. This is the wisdom of the early-19th century Danish existential philosopher Søren Kierkegaard, summed up in a playful, albeit bleakly realistic and exasperated, outburst in his masterpiece, *Either/Or*:

Marry, and you will regret it; don't marry, you will also regret it; marry or don't marry, you will regret it either way. Laugh at the world's foolishness, you will regret it; weep over it, you will regret that too; laugh at the world's foolishness or weep over it, you will regret both. Believe a woman, you will regret it; believe her not, you will also regret it... Hang yourself, you will regret it; do not hang yourself, and you will regret that too; hang yourself or don't hang yourself, you'll regret it either way; whether you hang yourself or do not hang yourself, you will regret both. This, gentlemen, is the essence of all philosophy.

We deserve pity; we will make disastrous decisions, we will form mistaken relationships, we will embark on misguided careers, we will invest our savings foolishly and we will spend years on friendships with unreliable and disappointing knaves. But we can we be consoled by a bitter truth: we have no better options, for the condition of existence is intrinsically rather than accidentally frustrating. Curiously, there is relief to be found in the knowledge of the inevitability of error and pain.

The mid-20th century English psychoanalyst Donald Winnicott, who specialised in working with parents and children, was disturbed by how often he encountered in his consulting rooms parents who were disappointed with themselves. They felt they were failing as parents and hated themselves intensely as a result. They were ashamed of their occasional rows, their bursts of short temper, their times of boredom around their own children and their many mistakes. They were haunted by a range of anxious questions: are we too strict, too lenient, too protective, not protective enough? What struck Winnicott, however, was that these people were almost never bad parents. They were loving, often very kind, and very interested in their children; they tried hard to meet their needs and to understand their problems as best they could. As parents, they were – as Winnicott put it in a memorable and important phrase – 'good enough'.

Winnicott identified a crucial issue. We often torment ourselves because we have in our minds a very demanding – and impossible – vision of what we're supposed to be like across a range of areas of our lives. This vision does not emerge from a careful study of what actual people are like; it is a fantasy, a punitive perfectionism, drawn from the cultural ether.

When it comes to parenting, we imagine a fantasy of parents who are always calm, always wise and always there when their child needs them. There are no parents like this. But a romantic conception of the perfect parent can fill our minds and make us anxious and fretful, because our own family life inevitably looks messy and muddled by comparison. Unreasonably inflated expectations leave us able to perceive only where we have fallen short.

With the phrase 'good enough', Winnicott was initiating a hugely important project. He wanted to move us away from idealisation. Ideals may sound nice, but they bring a terrible problem in their wake: they can make us despair of the quite good things we already do and have. 'Good enough' is a cure for the sickness of idealisation.

Winnicott introduced the idea of 'good enough' for parenting. But it applies widely across our lives, because we idealise cruelly about many different things. For example, we might refer to the 'good enough' job. It may not meet our fantasy demands: creative yet secure; fascinating yet unstressful; morally uplifting yet highly paid. But by the standards of what real jobs are like, it might be very decent and worth taking pride in. Or we could speak of the 'good enough' marriage. It might not be the perfect union of two souls, sex may be intermittent, there may be regular frustrations and misunderstandings and a fair number of flare-ups. But by the standards of actual long-term relationships, that might be genuine success.

By dialling down our expectations, the idea of 'good enough' resensitises us to the lesser, but very real, virtues we already possess, but that our unreal hopes have made us overlook. A 'good enough' life is not a bad life; it is the best existence that actual humans are ever likely to lead.

8
Diplomacy

Diplomacy is an art that evolved initially to deal with problems in the relationships between countries. The leaders of neighbouring states might be touchy on points of personal pride and quickly roused to anger. If they met head-on, they might be liable to infuriate each other and start a disastrous war. Instead, they learnt to send emissaries; people who could state things in less inflammatory ways, who wouldn't take the issues so personally and who could be more patient and emollient. Diplomacy was a way of avoiding the dangers that come from decisions formed in the heat of the moment. In their own palaces, two kings might be thumping the table and calling their rivals by abusive names, but in the quiet negotiating halls, the diplomat would say: 'My master is slightly disconcerted that...'

We still associate the term 'diplomacy' with embassies, international relations and high politics, but really it refers to a set of skills that matter in many areas of daily life, especially at the office and on the landing, outside the slammed doors of loved ones' bedrooms. Diplomacy is the art of advancing an idea or cause without unnecessarily inflaming passions or unleashing a catastrophe. It involves an understanding of the many facets of human nature that can undermine agreement and stoke conflict, and a commitment to unpicking these with foresight and grace.

The diplomat remembers, first and foremost, that some of the vehemence with which we can insist on having our way draws energy from an overall sense of not being respected within a relationship. We will fight with particular tenacity and apparent meanness over a so-called small point when we sense that the other person has failed to honour our wider need for appreciation and esteem. Behind our fierce way of arguing lies a frustrated plea for respect.

Diplomats know the intensity with which humans crave recognition. Therefore, although they may not always be able to agree with us, they take the trouble to show that they have bothered to see how things look through our eyes. They recognise that it is almost as important to people to feel heard as to win their case. We will put up with a lot once someone has demonstrated that they at least know how we feel. Diplomats put extraordinary effort into securing the health of the overall relationship so that smaller points can be conceded along the way without attracting feelings of untenable humiliation. They know how much a craving to be liked can stir beneath pitched fights over money or entitlements, schedules or procedures. They are careful to trade generously in emotional currency, so as not always to have to pay excessively in other, more practical, denominations.

Frequently, what is at stake within a negotiation with someone is a request that they change in some way: that they learn to be more punctual, or take more trouble on a task; that they be less defensive or more open-minded. The diplomat knows how futile it is to state these wishes too directly. They know the vast difference between having a correct diagnosis of how someone needs to grow and understanding a relevant way to help them do so. They know that what holds people back from evolution is fear. They therefore grasp that what we most need to offer to those whom we want to acknowledge difficult things is love and reassurance.

It helps greatly to know that those recommending change are not speaking from a position of impregnable perfection but are themselves wrestling with comparable demons in other areas. For a diagnosis not to sound like mere criticism, it helps for it to be delivered by someone with no compunctions to admitting to their own shortcomings. There can be few more successful pedagogic moves than to confess genially from the outset, 'And I am, of course, entirely mad as well...'

In negotiations, the diplomat is not addicted to indiscriminate or heroic truth-telling. They appreciate the legitimate place that minor lies can occupy in the service of greater truths. They know that if certain facts are emphasised, then the most important principles in a relationship may be forever undermined. Instead, they will enthusiastically say that the financial report or the homemade cake was very pleasing – not to deceive, but to affirm the truth of their overall attachment, which might be lost were a completely accurate account of their feelings laid out. Diplomats know that a small lie may be the guardian of a big truth. They appreciate their own resistance to the unvarnished facts, and privately hope that others may, on occasion, over certain matters, also take the trouble to lie to them without their knowledge.

Another trait of the diplomat is to be serene in the face of obviously bad behaviour: a sudden loss of temper, a wild accusation, a very mean remark. They don't take it personally, even when they are the target of rage. They reach instinctively for reasonable explanations and have clearly in their minds the better moments of a currently frantic but essentially loveable person. They know themselves well enough to understand that abandonments of perspective are both normal and almost always indicative of nothing much beyond exhaustion or passing despair. They do not aggravate a febrile situation through self-righteousness, which is a symptom of not knowing oneself too well. The person who bangs a fist on the table or announces extravagant opinions may simply be worried, frightened, or just very enthusiastic, conditions that should invite sympathy rather than disgust.

At the same time, the diplomat understands that there are moments to sidestep direct engagement. They do not try to teach a lesson whenever it might first or most apply: they wait until it has the best chance of being heard. At points, they disarm difficult people by reacting in unexpected ways. In the face of a tirade, instead of going on the defensive, the diplomatic person might suggest some lunch. When a harshly unfair criticism is launched at them, they might nod in partial agreement and declare that they have often said such things to themselves. They give a lot of ground away and avoid getting cornered in arguments that distract from the deeper issues. They remember the presence of a better version of the somewhat unfortunate individual currently on display.

The diplomat's reasonable tone is built, fundamentally on a base of deep pessimism. They know what the human animal is, and they understand how many problems might beset even a very good marriage, business, friendship or society. Their good-humoured way of greeting problems is a symptom of having swallowed a healthy measure of sadness from the outset. They have given up on the ideal, not out of weakness but out of a mature readiness to see compromise as a necessary requirement for getting by in a radically imperfect world.

The diplomat may be polite, but they are not averse to delivering bad news with uncommon frankness. Too often, we seek to preserve our image in the eyes of others by tiptoeing around harsh decisions, thereby make things worse than they need be. We should say that we're leaving them, that they're fired, that their pet project isn't going ahead, but we mutter instead that we're a little preoccupied at the moment, that we're delighted by their performance and that the plan is being actively discussed by the senior team. We mistake leaving some room for hope with kindness. But true niceness does not mean seeming nice; it means helping the people we are going to disappoint to adjust to reality as best they can. By administering a sharp, clean blow, the diplomatic person kills off the torture of hope, accepting the frustration that is likely to come their way. The diplomat is kind enough to let themselves be the target of hate.

The diplomat succeeds because they are a realist; they know we are inherently flawed, unreasonable, anxious, comedically absurd creatures who scatter blame unfairly, misdiagnose our pains and react appallingly to criticism, especially when it is accurate. Yet they are hopeful too, of the possibilities of progress when our disturbances have been properly factored in and cushioned with adequate reassurance, accurate interpretation and respect. Diplomacy seeks to teach us how many good things can be accomplished when we make accommodations for the crooked, sometimes touching and hugely unreliable material of human nature.

9
Effectiveness

It is one of the tragedies of our condition that we are measured not by the efforts we have invested, but by the results we can deliver. Good intentions are not enough. We may labour with determination for many decades and, in the end, have less to show for our work than someone who took swift and canny action over the course of a few clever months. In other words, we need not only to work hard, but to learn the art of effectiveness.

The effective person separates means and ends

The ancient Greek philosopher Aristotle was keen to distinguish means from ends. This sounds straightforward: on the one hand, there are our overarching goals, or ends; on the other, there are the methods, or means, we employ to try to achieve them. We can say we are effective when the means we employ truly do bring about the ends we are seeking.

However, in many important areas, it is difficult for us to select the means that will effectively deliver our goals. We cling to ideas of suitable means that betray our overall intentions. We know what we want but fall back on outdated, rigid means that have little chance of success. Suppose someone has been a bit lazy and unfocused and we want them to be more productive. The end is clear: getting their efforts back on track. Instinctively, we opt for a particular means: we give them a stern talking to. Intuitively this feels right. Yet our complaints and threats are liable to make the other person anxious and resentful and, as a consequence, less able to concentrate and think well. Or, in a dispute, our overarching end may be to bring another person over to our side. We want to convince them of our perspective and recruit them to our cause. Yet the means we adopt might involve attempting emphatically to prove that we are right and demonstrating with overwhelming force how very wrong and misguided they are. We may set about this with great intensity. As a result, the other person feels insulted and badgered; they resent us deeply and are determined not to acknowledge the merit of any of our points.

What marks out the effective person is that they care primarily about ends and are willing to be agnostic about means. They will do whatever works, even if the methods are not for a while in the spirit of their overall goal. They won't, for example, resent being patient, even if speed is their true end. They will make friends with an enemy, even when the victory of their side is what they are aiming for. They know how to employ humour and fool about with the team, even when they are deadly earnest about what they want to achieve.

The effective person doesn't mind how odd the means might initially sound. They don't mind biting their lip for a long while. It is only the end they keep in sight, like a trawler captain with a pilot light in a foggy sea.

The effective person asks themselves what they are really trying to do

The effective person brings a useful scepticism to the origination of their goals. They know how leaky and imprecise an organ the human mind is. Before taking action, they ask themselves a lot of questions about the purpose of their time on earth. They realise that their real aims might, upon inspection, be rather different from what they at first assumed. They see their initial desires as approximations, which may not yet be properly on target. They acknowledge that the mind doesn't necessarily reveal its true concerns instantly, and that it might be helpful to interrogate their desires over many quiet evenings to discover the deep longings that lie within them.

The effective person does not glamourise action

There is a deep allure to action. The busy person has prestige. To the nervous side of our minds, it can feel wise to get going. But the effective person has learnt to be unimpressed by mere effort. They know there is no special virtue in exaggerated displays of activity. It isn't because someone has been up at dawn or because their document is so long that he or she will win. Fortune favours the quiet thinkers who may, for a long time, have very little to show for their work. Effective people think a lot.

Effective people stare out of the window

We tend to reproach ourselves for staring out of the window. You are supposed to be 'working', or studying or ticking things off your to-do list. It can seem almost the definition of wasted time. It seems to produce nothing, to serve no purpose. We equate it with boredom, distraction, futility. The act of cupping your chin in your hands near a pane of glass and letting your eyes drift into the middle distance does not normally enjoy high prestige. We don't go around saying: 'I had a great day: the high point was staring out of the window.' But in a better society, maybe that's just the sort of thing truly effective people would say to one another.

Real work often doesn't look like work. The point of staring out of a window is, paradoxically, not to find out what is going on outside. It is, rather, an exercise in discovering the contents of our own minds. It is easy to imagine we know what we think, what we feel and what is going on in our heads. But we rarely do entirely. There's a huge amount of what makes us who we are that circulates unexplored and unused. Its potential lies untapped. It is shy and doesn't emerge under the pressure of direct questioning. If we do it right, staring out the window offers a way for us to listen out for the quieter suggestions and perspectives of our deeper selves.

Plato suggested a metaphor for the mind: our ideas are like birds fluttering around in the aviary of our brains. In order for the birds to settle, Plato understood that we needed periods of purpose-free calm. Staring out the window offers such an opportunity. We see the world going on: a patch of weeds is holding its own against the wind; a grey tower block looms through the drizzle. But we don't need to respond; we have no overarching intentions, and so the more tentative parts of ourselves have a chance to be heard, like the sound of church bells in the city once the traffic has died down at night.

The potential of daydreaming isn't recognised by societies obsessed with superficial productivity. Nonetheless, some of our greatest insights come when we stop trying to be purposeful and instead respect the creative potential of reverie. Daydreaming is a strategic rebellion against the excessive demands of immediate (but ultimately insignificant) pressures in favour of the diffuse, but very serious and effective, search for the wisdom of the unexplored deep self.

10
Eloquence

Eloquence is the attempt to get a set of tricky ideas into the mind of another person using the art of verbal charm. Managing employees requires eloquence; instilling ideas in children requires eloquence; and leading a country involves eloquence.

Unfortunately, the idea of 'eloquence' has acquired a bad name. If a book is charmingly written, if a song makes people want to dance, if a product is well marketed, if a person has a winning smile and sweet manners, suspicions develop only too easily.

However, the idea of eloquence is vital to any educational mission, for the ideas that we most need to hear are almost always the ones that we would in some ways like to ignore, and therefore need maximal help in absorbing. We need the toughest lessons to be coated in the most subtle and inventive charm. We need an alliance of education and eloquence.

We need eloquence because a central problem of the mind is that we know so much in theory about how we should behave and what we should do but engage so little with our knowledge in our day-to-day conduct. We know in theory about being punctual, about living by our values, about focusing on opportunities before it is too late, about being patient and open-hearted. Yet in practice, our wise ideas have a notoriously weak ability to motivate our actual behaviour. Our knowledge is both embedded within us and yet is ineffective for us.

Although eloquence is associated with the use of fancy words and the ability to speak without notes, it is really the close study of how to get a message to live in the minds of an audience.

It builds on the grim realisation that stating our case logically and accurately often won't be enough.

The idea of eloquence was investigated with particular acuity by the philosopher Aristotle in Athens around the middle of the 4th century BCE. Aristotle saw how often a weak argument could triumph in public debate while a far more sensible proposal was ignored. He didn't think this was because the listeners were stupid but because of how large a role our emotions play in determining the way that people react to what is said and to who says it.

When the wrong emotions are stimulated, we have demagoguery, which employs eloquence in the service of a sinister objective. But if we admit – and fear – how powerful this can be, we are implicitly recognising the possibility of, and need for, a better alternative: a way of speaking that can be equally emotionally intelligent, yet aim at goodness. Aristotle did not want noble-minded people to stop trying to be eloquent; he wanted to give them the same weapons as the crooked. He dreaded a world in which people of ill intent would know how to stir the emotions, while serious, thoughtful people stuck to plain facts. A number of his lectures therefore investigated the art of eloquence, and gave birth to a philosophical tradition of studying how best to speak in order to be truly heard.

A number of moves suggest themselves. For a start, we should take care to humanise ourselves in the eyes of those we are addressing. Our instinct might be to try to bolster our prestige and stress our seniority and authority, so as to open the ears of the audience. But we are typically facing another problem altogether: the audience is at risk of not engaging with what we say because they suspect that we are remote, from another world, cold to their real concerns and perhaps even privately looking down on them. The eloquent move is therefore to signal our common humanity. We can make a self-deprecating joke, confess to a slightly shameful anxiety or talk about the very boring and ordinary events that unfolded for us at the weekend. We indicate that we too are flawed, worried, put-upon and sometimes sad. We emphasise shared experience so that some of the tricky and unusual things we need to say feel as if they emerge from the mind of someone sympathetic and relatable, not a distant automaton. The need to come across as ordinary is never more important than when one isn't quite.

Eloquence also remembers the need to give a sensory, emotionally powerful form to our ideas. In 1894, the prominent English writer Thomas Hardy set out to transform public attitudes as to who should have access to education, which at that time was largely open only to the well-to-do. He might have produced a polemical lecture or a statistic-rich essay stressing the potential benefits of education to the economy or making a general case for social justice. But he knew how our minds work, and how little appetite we have to be hectored. He understood how facts and numbers can leave us cold, and how many worthy causes have died because they were articulated in a language dead to the needs of the heart.

Therefore, Hardy made a move the applicability of which stretches way beyond his particular example: he wrote a novel that we know today as *Jude the Obscure*. It tells the story of one very particular person, Jude Fawley, a stonemason whose ambitions to study at university are cruelly thwarted. Hardy spends a lot of time describing Jude and his life; he tells us about what Jude was like as a child and how his aspirations developed. He tells us about the clothes Jude wears and what the sky is like when he goes for a walk in the evening. He gives us the precise terms of Jude's rejection in a letter from the head of the college where he had hoped to study:

> Sir,—I have read your letter with interest; and, judging from your description of yourself as a working-man, I venture to think that you will have a much better chance of success in life by remaining in your own sphere and sticking to your trade than by adopting any other course. That, therefore, is what I advise you to do.

By this point we are probably in tears and desperate to help bring a better world into existence. Hardy makes his case eloquent – that is, emotionally powerful – by keeping in mind that our sympathies are aroused more by the cases of people we feel we know than by abstract argument. Hardy knows that we must have a visceral sense of the truth of an idea, not just be brow-beaten into accepting it.

Without any aspirations to being a great writer, we can learn from this example. We can grasp that what we are battling is often not so much ignorance as indifference. It is easy enough to share information; it is another, altogether trickier, task to persuade an audience to care. The skills this requires lie in an area almost always overlooked by public speakers: art.

Art may be most usefully defined as the discipline devoted to trying to get concepts creatively into people's heads. The ablest speakers never assume that the bare bones of a story can be enough to win over their audience. They will not suppose that an idea or a committee meeting or a new piece of technology must in and of itself carry some intrinsic degree of interest that will cause the audience to be immediately moved or motivated. These artists of words know that no event, however striking, can ever guarantee involvement. For this latter prize, they must work harder, practising their distinctive craft, which means paying attention to language, alighting on animating details and keeping a tight rein on pace and structure.

Eloquence is a solution to a basic problem: our minds are sieve-like, we retain little; we are easily distracted, our emotions quickly overpower our intellect; envy, fear and suspicion readily turn us against the views of others; our sympathy is moved more by individual cases than by abstract issues. To ensure that a message is properly received and retained, we must acknowledge the peculiarities of our minds. It is not enough to be accurate, concise and logical. We need to do that trickier thing: touch the well-hidden chords of the heart.

11
Empathy

Empathy requires us to draw on often hidden parts of ourselves to shed light onto the characters of people who might seem very different from us in class, status or time.
__John Singer Sargent, *Lord Ribblesdale*, 1902.

We know that empathy is an important quality that enables us to see the world as it looks through other, normally very different, eyes. But we may be unsure quite how to achieve this prized perspective.

We may think of it as the business of escaping our normal egoism, of leaving the self, and putting ourselves imaginatively into someone else's experience. But the trick to empathy might be slightly different. It isn't so much about transcending ourselves as it is about practising an unusual kind of introspection, which takes us into less familiar parts of our own minds.

For example, imagine if we were asked to empathise with the formally dressed man, Lord Ribblesdale, staring at us from this portrait by the American artist John Singer Sargent. Our first feeling is likely to be that the man looks utterly foreign to us: aristocratic, haughty and contemptuous, a figure to whom we have not the slightest connection or relationship.

But the necessary manoeuvre is to try to draw on certain, less obvious, parts of our own experience. Insofar as each of us contains, in latent form, all of human life, there will inevitably be a small, currently recessive, part of us that is in sync with the mindset we associate with a 19th-century aristocrat.

We might remember one day being on a busy train, jostled by groups of rowdy, perhaps drunk, fellow passengers. The mood might not have lasted, but we might recognise for an instant in ourselves a potential to look rather sternly at others and suspect that, in some ways, we might be rather better than them. Or maybe there was a time when we were eight and our parents were in the hallway about to go out to a formal party, and we tried on their smart coats or jackets and loved the feeling of authority that comes from certain kinds of formal clothing. We may generally have a very casual style and a democratic spirit, but locked away in our minds is the potential to grasp what might be appealing about looking grand and facing the world down with a stern demeanour. In trying to empathise with a lord, we're seeking out and detecting an overlap of experience. We're learning to recognise in a very different person an echo of our own intimate history.

The person who lacks empathy isn't so much selfish as not fully alive to the darker, less familiar, more weird recesses of themselves. These are the parts that are a range of things that they aren't most of the time; the subordinate bits that are, in secret, a little aristocratic, surprisingly male or female, a thief or a child, when society expects them to be merely democratic, a man, a woman, a law-abiding citizen or an adult. The unempathetic person isn't refusing the challenge of entering into the mind of another person; they are wary of treading with sufficient imagination into their own consciousness.

Behind the reserve of the unempathetic is a fear of running into troubling emotions. They may be confident, yet don't engage with memories of what it was like to stutter and be lost in the early years. They are successful, but put aside the anguished apprehensions of rejection and failure that sometimes come in nightmares and would connect them with some of the people they walk contemptuously past in the streets. The long-married person harbours a promiscuous single self they pretend not to recognise. In the life of the quiet,

_____ Behind the reserve of the unempathetic is a fear of running into troubling emotions.

serious individual there will have been moments, quickly forgotten, when they felt like throwing their books into the river and swearing at their teacher. We contain multitudes within us that we don't dare to know. The opposite of empathy isn't just thinking of yourself; it is thinking of yourself in limited ways.

An impressive feature of many legal systems is that someone who has been accused of a crime is entitled to have a skilled and sophisticated advocate argue their case before the judge and jury. The defence lawyer doesn't need to like their client or think them innocent; their task isn't to lie or deceive, but to construct the most favourable interpretation that the facts allow. Perhaps their client did indeed steal some money, but they felt very frightened; they didn't mean to take quite so much; they'd just received some terrible news. The advocate searches in the surrounding circumstances for whatever mitigating factors there might be.

The exercise has far wider applicability than a courtroom. Normally, we only ever get 'hired' – as it were – by ourselves. We are geniuses at representing our own side, at finding excuses and extenuating circumstances for what we have done or not done. When it comes to others, we typically act like the most aggressive and forensic prosecution; we in effect deny that someone could be at once good and have acted in a particularly disheartening way.

There could be another approach. The empathetic person makes it their business to adopt, in a wide variety of situations, the outlook of the other's defence lawyer. They perform a hugely unfamiliar and often uncomfortable exercise: they do whatever is in their power to make their adversaries seem – for a time – reasonable and motivated by a comprehensible set of arguments. They hold back their normal instincts and try to apply a generous construction on the motives involved.

Empathy needn't mean we end up thinking the other person is saintly. We might still conclude that they are, for instance, not to be trusted, that they shouldn't get the job or that we'd definitely better not marry them (just as in a court case, the aim is to arrive at justice, not to acquit every defendant). But the deeper result is that we don't merely see the other as a caricature. We understand how they came to be the way they are and recognise along the way, if we are frank, how many of their less than lovely qualities we share.

It is only too easy to judge harshly when we do not deploy the correct degree of self-knowledge. One day, when we put the heating up higher than they would like, our partner may become agitated. They may start to shout and we, just as quickly, may – with a degree of self-satisfaction – start to think of them as 'insane'. It may be that we have never had this precise over-wrought reaction to heating, but if we were correctly empathetic, we would be aware of the many occasions when we ourselves became surprisingly worked up about things that don't seem very important to others. Truly empathetic people suspect that there are few kinds of madnesses of which they couldn't, in certain circumstances, be capable, and are accordingly humble.

The more we bring our knowledge of ourselves to bear

on others, the richer our insights into them become. We start to know their deeper secrets and wishes, without asking. If we encounter someone who is always joking and seems very cheery, the empathetic person keeps in mind – because they know so well how they have been in certain of their own manic moods – that this ebullience almost certainly masks a sad and hurt aspect. They sense this because they can recall moments from their own experience when they adopted a brave and positive manner precisely when they felt close to collapse.

Bringing our experience to bear matters immensely in commercial situations. What we call good service is, in essence, the fruit of empathy. When a waiter hovers at the table and asks repeatedly if everyone is having a nice time, it is because they have failed to factor in their own experience of irritation at overly ingratiating attention.

The world of design is filled with absences of empathy. The planners of paths around parks, for instance, routinely forget how people actually walk.

When they lay out their paths, they forget our impatience when faced with any slightly longer route, because they have failed to consult with their own selves. They mess up their work because they cease to think of themselves as their own first customers.

Empathy is often framed as a moral duty and interpreted as directly opposed to self-interest. In order to be more empathetic, the line goes, we should abandon our own personal well-being and success. But this call to greater empathy more or less ensures its

A lack of empathy on the part of park designers means they forget how impatient people can be to take the shortest route.

own failure. Our ingrained need to look after ourselves will reliably triumph.

A more accurate understanding of empathy doesn't see it as opposed to our own interests. The reality is that we are often hampered and derailed in our projects because we are not empathetic enough, not sensitive enough to what is going on for the people we're trying to do things with, or to whom we aim to sell our services. Empathy is an essential resource for doing what we want more successfully, which captures a fundamental hope of civilisation: that being good should not be the enemy of prosperity.

12
Entrepreneurship

The modern world is in love with entrepreneurship. Starting your own business holds the same sort of prestige as, in previous ages, making a pilgrimage to Jerusalem or spearing multiple enemies in battle.

However, what it takes to be a successful entrepreneur remains maddeningly elusive. Governments and public bodies do their best to encourage people by helping out with the practicalities: offering tax breaks, making failure less punitive, setting up 'enterprise zones' and so on. Yet at the heart of successful entrepreneurship lies something more abstract: an accurate insight into the causes of human unhappiness. Every morally minded business in some way alleviates a particular kind of suffering.

Because consumer society is now well developed, it can be easy to assume that everything must already have been done to please and satiate the audience; that every possible gimmick and thrill has been amply explored and that we have far too much stuff already. These concerns may meld with ecological concern about the planet's diminishing resources to create a view that we should henceforth aim for less and that capitalism is done for.

However, the theory that we have come to the end of the road of entrepreneurial innovation, that everything has already been done, is conceptually impossible. The clearest evidence for this claim is that most people are still very unhappy in all sorts of fascinating (and, in this context, inspiring) ways. Cheeringly for the entrepreneurial among us, the frustrations, irritations and griefs of the present are an inexhaustible source of raw materials out of which the businesses of the future can be built.

To get a measure of just how many new businesses still have to be invented – and therefore how much further capitalism has to develop – we need only take an average day and focus on how much annoys us and how much satisfies us, from the moment we wake up to the time we fall back to sleep. Areas where we are fairly happy are those where further developments seem unnecessary. The market is evidently saturated and new entrants will face a high degree of competition that will depress wages and profitability for all players. Conversely, areas of dissatisfaction are, in essence, zones of unexplored opportunity. The greater the unhappiness, the bigger the potential market. Let's imagine the things about which we might feel quite happy in a typical day:

- Breakfast cereal: there is a huge choice, many of them delicious. Even the healthy ones have become satisfying as well as nutritious.
- Mobile phones: we get clear reception and are connected to a distant continent in a heartbeat. Things are working well here.
- Coffee: yet another outlet has opened nearby. The milk is perfect, the beans subtle and beguiling.
- Clothes: thirty-two different kinds of T-shirt are offered at very reasonable prices. All the possibilities and permutations in this area have been explored.

But there is plenty more to frustrate and depress us at other points in a typical day:

- An argument with our partner: it's hard to know quite what is going on. This is the third one this week. Why is it so hard to live together?

- Anxiety on the way into work: is our career on track? What are we doing this for? What happened to our youthful promise?

- The children complaining about their homework again: bored and listless.

- Disgusting new block of flats going up at the end of the road: who did this? Why are they going to be so expensive?

- Beautiful restaurant but conversation with client sagging and dull. Why is it so hard to know what to talk about?

- Hard to calm down in the evening. Best to get a little drunk and check phone – a lot.

One could go on; our griefs and irritations might fill dozens of pages. But already from the briefest sketch, we can discern the shape of some significant new businesses that might be pioneered in the future. For example: a therapeutic service to help couples in crisis. Given the importance of relationships compared with the relatively minor role occupied by luxury transport, the business could theoretically exceed the revenues of a car company in a short time. A career counselling service would be just as necessary, one that worked properly, that was pleasant to visit, intelligently delivered, based on real science and that aimed to deliver clients with a vision of how to unite their talent with the needs of the world. A new kind of school: ideally, this would work back from the real problems of life in order to teach people things they actually need to know, rather than forcing them through arcane scholastic exercises. A property development firm that accepts profits of 5% p.a. (rather than the usual 25%+) and that sets out to build efficient, beautiful houses. A mobile phone app designed to teach people how to have better conversations rather than merely allowing them to have further conversations of the uninspiring kind they already have. A new kind of monastery, without religion, offering calm and retreat to those ground down by the tempests of modern life...

Everywhere we look, there are frustrations. Every one of them is, in theory, the seed of an enterprise. A first step towards entrepreneurship is hence to learn to study our own unhappiness and register all our pulses of distress, however minor. Declining profits are merely symptoms of giant failures of imagination on the part of the business community. Too many people throw themselves at the same area because they can't think of anything more innovative to do than to start yet another airline, mobile phone company or supermarket chain, to the distress of all participants. By contrast, healthy profits are a reward for understanding and mastering a given human need ahead of others.

Ideas are not enough, of course. There always comes the need to take care of practicalities and money; the requirement to raise loans, convince investors and find partners. But none of these practical steps stand any chance of working out if the original, psychological insight isn't sound. By the same token, if the insight is razor-sharp and truly tailored to human functioning, then, however arduous the journey, the business will stand a high chance of benefiting humanity and making money, too.

13
Innovation

Business is committed to satisfying the appetites of customers, which tends to mean the appetites they have revealed to date. In the politics of the office, raising suggestions that deviate from present patterns of consumption can put an innovative mind in a vulnerable position. It explains the dogged adherence to mediocre offerings and the frequency with which avenues of pleasure and satisfaction go unexplored and opportunities for growth are set aside.

The idea of pleasing customers is not in dispute. What can be targeted, however, is the mistaken assumption – operating in the background of much of commercial life – that what people want is a fixed factor, when it is in fact dramatically malleable, contingent and divergent. The most powerful and charming proof of this lies in the history of culture, which repeatedly shows us that, with the right encouragement, large groups of people can become highly sensitive to features that go unnoticed in other societies or eras. Culture demonstrates that there are far fewer limits to what we can be led to appreciate than we might imagine.

Take rocks, for instance. In 826 CE, during China's Tang dynasty, a middle-aged civil servant, Bai Juyi, was taking a stroll around Lake Tai in eastern China when his eye was caught by a pair of large, oddly shaped but distinctly pleasing rocks. So struck was he by their form, full of ancient nobility and endurance, that he had them shipped back to his home. He wrote a poem about them, 'A Pair of Rocks', now one of the most well-known works in Chinese literature.

Bai Juyi admitted that his rocks were not typically beautiful; they were worn and dark and their undersides distinctly mossy. But

The distinctive, glossy forms of Lingbi rock were especially prized among the wealthy, cultivated Chinese people of the Tang dynasty. If our attention is guided in the right way, there are many things we could come to honour and appreciate that are currently overlooked.

in their own way, the rocks seemed eloquent bearers of the tenets of Daoism, which urges us to keep the mighty forces of the universe constantly in mind and to accommodate ourselves serenely to their demands. Bai Juyi had the rocks placed on his desk so he could be inspired by their suggestions of equanimity and patience.

> Turning my head around, I ask the pair of rocks:
> 'Can you keep company with an old man like myself?'
> Although the rocks cannot speak,
> They promise that we will be three friends.

Bai Juyi's advocacy set off a wave of enthusiasm and was the foundation of an important new sector in China's artistic economy. Stones began to be tracked down in the most inaccessible places. They were mounted on wooden bases, traded for large sums and installed around the houses of the wealthy. Cultivated people were expected to have an appreciation of gongshi, or spirit stones, which were valued as highly as any painting or calligraphic scroll. The most favoured rocks were the dark glossy kind quarried from the limestone of Lingbi, in the northern Anhui province. The best examples might cost as much as a house.

In the first decade of the 12th century, a civil servant, Mi Fu, was appointed magistrate in Huaiyang province. On arrival at his official residence he attended a formal meeting with all the administrators of the region. They stood waiting for him in the front garden in a position of solemn reverence, but as he walked towards

This painting portrays a
key moment in China's cultural
history: the importance of
revering natural forces.
__Guo Xu, *Mi Fu and Elder
Brother Rock*, 1503.

them, Mi Fu committed a sudden and shocking breach of protocol. His gaze was diverted by an unusually large and interesting rock in the garden. Instead of offering his respects to his hosts, Mi Fu bowed ceremoniously to the rock, addressed it as 'Elder Brother' and made an elaborate speech in its honour. Only after fully expressing his devotion did Mi Fu turn to his flabbergasted hosts and say hello. Using this incident to celebrate the wisdom of showing respect for natural forces rather than paying heed to social etiquette, China's painters made the moment central to the Chinese artistic canon – akin to the significance of the Annunciation in the Western tradition.

The love of rocks, and the birth of an economy to support it, is not solely a Chinese phenomenon. For centuries, the village of Etretat in Normandy had been impoverished and ignored. The small community survived on fishing and collecting iodine-rich kelp from the shoreline. Then, in the early 1880s, the painter Claude Monet stopped by and noted some remarkable cliff formations around the village, especially three natural arches and a needle carved out by the sea. He made more than sixty paintings of the cliffs. He was fascinated by their appearance at different times of day, and liked to record how the waves mounted their fury around the needle while halos of light collected in dizzying shapes around the arches.

Monet's work helped to transform Etretat. A train line was laid down from Le Havre to cater for the continuous stream of visitors who wanted to see for themselves what the great impressionist had appreciated in the village. Hotels sprang up around the region. Within

Monet devotedly painted scenes of a part of Normandy coastline that had never received artistic attention before.
__Claude Monet, *La Manneporte près d'Etretat*, 1886.

a few year of Monet's depictions, ten thousand visitors a month were coming to Etretat in the summer months, renting rooms and buying ice creams, deckchairs and postcards. The artist had, inadvertently, given rise to an industry.

Our culture can well understand the role of sensitivity around the arts; it has perhaps not yet fully grasped its importance in relation to entrepreneurship. Because business involves a host of financial and managerial efforts that may seem quite remote, from the shadows on the cliffs of Etretat or the veins across the black polished surfaces of the rocks of Lingbi, one can forget that it is often ultimately orbiting an original aesthetic insight. A lot of what we term 'business' is the commodification of a moment of pleasure. Artists and entrepreneurs may seem to be entirely different human types, but their work starts from the same crucial base: an acute sensitivity that has been respected and ambitiously brought to the attention of others.

The rocks of Lingbi and the cliffs of Etretat remind us how much we have yet to open our eyes to; how much that imposing category 'what customers want' remains open to advocacy, waiting for us to have the courage of our pleasures. One of the big tasks of civilisation is to teach us how to better enjoy life. The romantic assumption is that we know this intuitively and all we need is greater freedom to follow our instincts. The classical picture is that a pleasant life is, in fact, a deliberate accomplishment. It is a rational achievement that builds on careful examination of experience and involves deliberate strategies to guide us more reliably to the things that truly please us.

In this, business is not the enemy; it is the commodifying, arranging, systematising tool by which the things we enjoy can be more reliably sampled.

At various points in the past, charming little things have come into focus, been taken up by the commercial forces of the world and turned into universal and easily recognised pleasures. The idea of eating small pieces of pasta twisted into spirals must once have seemed strange and hard to take seriously – if you had to make your own, almost no one would ever eat them. But they have been taken up by industrialists and advertisers and recipe book publishers and TV chefs, and now millions of packets of fusilli are sold in supermarkets every week around the planet. The leading manufacturer, the Barilla Group, has an annual turnover of €3.3 billion.

In Japan, much attention is paid to the blossoming of cherry trees. Almost everyone makes a special trip to see them at their best, taking special picnics to eat under the white flowers. The boost to the economy is the equivalent of around a trillion yen (around £6 billion or $8.5 billion). The UK has very nice cherry trees too, but has not yet developed a portion of the economy around them. Consequently, although people in Skegness and Taunton like cherry trees, they don't pay special attention to them; most people find the season has passed before they have noticed. Building a pleasure into the economy isn't a good thing primarily because it can make money; when an industry gets organised, it raises the status of a pleasure and brings it more reliably and impressively to our notice.

There are so many small pleasures whose potential has

not yet been fully grasped by society at large: walking at midnight; looking at moss growing on old walls; having a proper conversation with a stranger... The idea that these pleasures might sponsor large industries devoted to promoting them sounds odd only because they are not yet established. The activities in themselves are no less pleasurable than sliding down the side of a mountain (the skiing industry contributes £42 billion or $60 billion to the world economy each year) or watching people hit a small ball over a net (the tennis market is worth £1 billion or $1.5 billion a year). A few decades ago, a prediction that these enjoyments would flourish on such a scale might have seemed absurd. There are vast industries waiting to emerge around all the things we could enjoy and benefit from, but don't as yet because we have not been encouraged to pay attention to their charms.

14
Leadership

When people emigrated from Europe to the New World, in the 19th century, they knew that they would probably never see their old friends again. They were taking a step with major consequences; they were acutely conscious of the scale of what they were doing. They had sold their cottage, they had packed up all their belongings, they could feel the slow movement of the ship. They had a fourteen-week journey before them; they knew there was no going back

There are many steps in life that have a similar character; they take us to a new world from which we can't return. However, they are usually less overtly dramatic, so the trauma is not as easily recognised, even though we suffer just the same.

Ascending to a leadership position is one such example. To become a leader is to undergo a profound change. Some earlier (and very nice) versions of oneself will have to be packed away. The sarcastic genius may not be coming back. The people you used to share a lot of good times with at work will think you've altered for the worse and become more distant; you won't be such fun to be around. You will seem colder. You will lack a sense of humour. There is no other way. You will have to function without being understood by those you used to be close to.

To be a good leader, you will need to be both an ordinary worker and someone removed and a little otherworldly. Irrespective of one's religious beliefs, it is clear that Jesus was one of the great leaders of all time. He united two characteristics that generally seem opposed: he was powerful and he was normal. The central idea of Christianity is that Jesus is the son of God but, at the same time, one

_____ To become a leader is to undergo a profound change.

of us. The stories of the life of Jesus stress how normal and down to earth he was in many ways. His parents weren't well off. He worked in his father's carpentry shop until he was thirty. One story recounts how some of his supporters were making a long journey on foot to a place called Emmaus. Jesus joins them, in disguise. They chat with him; they talk about many things. They think he's just an ordinary, interesting man. It's only when they reach their destination and have a meal, and Jesus blesses the bread in his special, characteristic way, that they recognise him.

The great sellers of religion, like the Baroque painter Caravaggio, loved this story. They realised what a key selling point the ordinariness of Jesus was. You could sit down and have a meal with him. He had the same kind of worries and troubles as you. He understood you; he knew what your life was like. The idea was that Jesus won the trust and loyalty of his followers at a very personal level; he didn't simply impose or assert his superiority.

The Jesus-type role (being both 'above' and 'with') is demanded by the modern workplace. A common complaint about leadership is that the leader doesn't understand, or has forgotten, or doesn't care about what it is like for those lower down the system.

When she takes public transport, the Queen of England is at one level doing a very normal thing. But when she does it, it becomes astonishing – because she could travel by helicopter; because she is the woman who, in Westminster Abbey, was crowned Queen of Great Britain, Ireland and the British Dominions beyond the sea, defender of the realm and of the faith.

Jesus was an unparallelled
leader because he combined
greatness with ordinariness.
__Caravaggio, *The Supper
at Emmaus*, 1601.

Now she's on the bus in the seat next to us. What touches us, even if we don't usually spell it out, is that she is both sovereign and passenger at the same time; at once extraordinary and normal.

Hierarchy is a painful aspect of human society. There are good reasons why wholesale equality isn't practical, but the longing for influential figures to demonstrate understanding and sympathy towards the less powerful runs deep. That's why it is moving and reassuring if we see someone who could fly by helicopter take the train. It bodes well for the world.

We live in societies that are officially egalitarian and meritocratic, yet we are endlessly exposed to massive differences in wealth, power, status and fame. We are fascinated by the lives of people at the top, yet we are troubled too. Do they understand? Do they know what it's like? Any hints that they do are significant.

When the Queen takes the bus, she is bridging the world of history, grandeur, money and power with everyday life. The cynical (or ambitious) person might say that there should only be equals in our societies. But as this is unlikely to happen any time soon, what we desperately need is people at the top who understand their responsibilities towards the many.

Another tricky aspect of leadership is that we will, in certain ways, need to adopt a parental perspective. The notion of parenthood is easy to mock and make the target of scepticism. When, in 1964, Bob Dylan sang to a generation of parents that 'your sons and your daughters are beyond your command' ('The Times They Are a- Changin''), he was counting on recognition of the failings of parental authority.

Top: Queen Elizabeth II
aboard a different kind
of coach to the one we
would normally associate
her with.

Bottom: Queen Elizabeth II
at her coronation in 1953.

The difficulty of parenthood is being asked to be the guardian of the long-term interests of someone who will be convinced, on multiple occasions, that one is deeply and viciously wrong (about the computer, the sleepover, the car use...). And, indeed, one may be, which doesn't preclude the need to come up with a plan and a principle.

It is always a surprise to a new parent how much they can love their child and also how weird it is to have to say 'no' to them, and then be the target of special hatred by someone they would lay down their life for. The role of a parent is a training ground in the inevitability of making unpopular decisions, and in not expecting sympathy or gratitude for a very long time. It might be twenty-five years until your child understands why you made a certain decision, let alone acknowledges that there might have been a point to it.

Modern leaders and modern parents aren't inclined to draw parallels between their activities; to think that 'my children are my employees' and 'my employees are my children'. Yet it is because of our squeamishness that we don't see domestic life as the training for the office (and for leadership roles especially) that it might be. There are MBAs to be earned at the kitchen table and honed amid the anguished screams around bedtime and teeth-brushing.

We tend to understate the negatives of major developments in life. Weddings generally exaggerate the joys of coupledom, and typically only the fulfilling and exciting aspects of becoming a parent are discussed. It's not that there are no good points, of course; it's just that on their own they give an unrealistic account of what we are

_____ A tricky aspect of leadership is that we will need to adopt a parental perspective.

getting into. They raise expectations too high. By comparison, being married or being a parent is a let-down. The risk is that we become disenchanted and panicky when things turn out to be tougher than we had anticipated.

The position of being the boss, joining the leadership team, or generally having more responsibility and power seems enviable. But considerable difficulties and troubles come with it too. We need to accept that leadership will involve leaving behind a lot for which we will, in time, grow nostalgic.

15
Objectivity

Our brains are brilliant instruments; able to reason, synthesise, remember and imagine at an extraordinary pitch and rate. We trust them immediately and innately – and have reason to be proud of them too.

However, these brains – let's call them walnuts, in honour of their appearance – are also very subtly and dangerously flawed machines. They are defective in ways that typically don't announce themselves to us and therefore give us few clues as to how vigilant we should be about our mental processes. Most of the walnut's flaws can be attributed to the way the instrument evolved over millions of years. It adapted to deal with threats, some of which are no longer with us. At the same time, it had no chance to develop adequate responses to myriad challenges generated by our own complex societies. We should feel pity for its situation and compassion for ourselves.

Remaining more or less objective requires us to adopt a focused and ongoing scepticism towards a great many of the ideas, schemes, plans and feelings generated by the faulty walnut that stands at the top of our spinal column. Here are just some of the many things we need to watch out for.

The walnut is influenced by the body to an extent it doesn't recognise

The walnut is extremely bad at understanding why it is having certain thoughts and ideas. It tends always to attribute them to rational, objective conditions out in the world, rather than seeing that they might be stemming from the impact of the body upon its thought processes. It doesn't typically notice the role that levels of sleep, sugar, hormones and other bodily factors play upon the formation of ideas. The walnut adheres to a psychological interpretation of plans and positions that are frequently merely physiological. Therefore, it can feel certain that the right answer is to divorce the spouse or leave the job rather than go back to bed or eat something to raise blood sugar levels.

The walnut is influenced by its past, but can't see its own projections

The walnut believes it judges each new situation on its own merits, but it inevitably draws upon patterns of action and feeling shaped in previous years. This saves time, and has real evolutionary advantages. However, many situations in the present are deceptive, resembling the past only enough to trigger a familiar response while in fact having many unique characteristics that get overlooked. At moments of ambiguity, the walnut can jump to some catastrophic conclusions. It might, for example, assume that any older man who speaks confidently is out to humiliate them, when actually it was just one man – their father – who did this. Or it will find it hard to get close to all women because one specific woman was a source of trauma between the ages of one and ten. It is understandable, but very regrettable.

The walnut doesn't like to stop and think

The walnut evolved for rapid, instinctive decision-making, and has a hard time stepping back to address what we might term the first-order questions. It will always be keener to do than reflect; to act rather than analyse. Remember that philosophy is, at best, two thousand years old. We prefer to keep running a business the way it has always been run rather than stop and ask: what would it mean to properly help our customers? We rush to book a holiday rather than pause and reflect on what we really enjoyed about past trips. We form an ambition to break into journalism because we enjoy being 'creative' rather than analysing the component parts of our interests. Hence we miss our own vagueness, inconsistency and confusion.

So bad is the walnut at thinking, it often needs another walnut nearby to help it. Thinking generates anxiety and a desire to run fast in the opposite direction because of the difficult truths the walnut might unearth. But in the presence of another walnut, we can't bolt so easily. That is why philosophy started as a conversation and psychoanalysis depends on two people unpacking one person's thoughts and associations.

Sadly, we rarely call on other walnuts to help us analyse, and usually pass the time chatting idly about sport or the latest celebrity scandal. In short, the walnut is very good at seeing what others are up to, but finds it hard to have a clear perception of itself. It can take it thirty years to gradually gain an insight that was obvious to a stranger within two minutes. The walnut seems to be a machine that is not designed to look at itself (just as our eyes can't see the middle of our backs).

_____ It can take thirty years to gradually gain an insight that was obvious to a stranger within two minutes.

The walnut is bad at self-control and gets passionate about, and scared of, the wrong things

The walnut constantly gets excited about things that aren't good for it: sugar, salt and sex with strangers, for a start. Advertising knows how to exploit this cognitive frailty to perfection. Our confusions can generally be traced back to targets that would once have been crucial and fitting for us to focus on. Our desires used to be reliable in simpler environments, but cause chaos in the complicated conditions of modernity. The same holds true for our fears: in the past, fears were bound to things that could kill us. Fears were a good idea to get us out of genuine danger. But nowadays, many things excite our fear systems without there being any real threat. We have panic attacks before speaking in public for no good reason; at the same time, the real threats of modernity (global warming or another sub-prime mortgage financial crisis) evade our detection radars entirely.

The walnut is egocentric, not polycentric

The walnut is primed to look at things from its own point of view. It often can't believe that there are other ways of considering an issue. Other people can therefore seem perverse or horrible to it, sparking outrage or self-pity. It's only in the last second, from an evolutionary point of view, that the walnut has started to try to imagine what it might be like to be someone else (a symptom of this is that it has learnt to take pleasure in novels). But this empathetic capacity is still fragile and tends to collapse, especially when the walnut is tired and someone is trying to persuade it of a strange-sounding idea.

The walnut is intellectually squeamish

The walnut doesn't like uncomfortable information. It doesn't want to hear about problems. It looks out for information that confirms its biases and choices. It hates being the devil's advocate. It favours short-term comfort over long-term growth and evolution. If confronted with a disquieting fact, it will tend to repress or skirt around it. The walnut places self-protection far above truth.

The walnut is not an independent thinker

The walnut grew up depending on the mood of the group or clan for survival. It is therefore highly primed to fit in with common sense and prevailing opinion. It doesn't generally like to use itself as a source of original data or insight. Other people's opinions matter hugely, irrespective of how foolish they might be. Because we came from small groups, one or two compliments can delight us; one criticism can sow panic. This is tricky in a wired age. We become hypersensitive to what an absurdly small number of other people happen to believe.

The walnut misunderstands causality

The walnut used to think it might have been responsible for the lightning in the sky and that earthquakes were a result of its own bad thoughts and deeds. It took a while to overcome that skewed perspective. But the walnut still projects personal dynamics and overproduces generalities based on things that have happened to it: it stays trapped by personal, rather than statistical or objective, experience.

Being more vigilant about the flaws in our walnuts gives us a range of important advantages in our search for objectivity:

- we become better at noticing the potential for errors in our own judgement and therefore stand a higher chance of preventing them. We can only start to avoid mistakes when we know mistakes are an active possibility.

- when we deal with other people, we can ask ourselves whether they might be acting from a walnut flaw, but not know it. This will make us both bolder about disagreeing with them and also kinder and more generous in the face of their less than sensible behaviours.

- when we deal with large groups of people, we can be aware that the walnut does very weird things in packs – but that's OK, and there's no reason to panic if we find our ideas meet with resistance.

At heart, compensating for the faulty equipment that nature has given us is the task of what we call education, culture and civilisation. The flaws in the walnut are also what makes it imperative that we try to act with kindness and tolerance. We should go easy on ourselves and others: we are trying to do some very difficult things around one another, with the use of a highly troublesome and only intermittently accurate tool.

16
Playfulness

_____ When a child is being playful, they are liberated from the fear of error.

We are the inheritors of a view of life that may be called 'bourgeois' in honour of its most ambitious advocates. It sees work and play as radically distinct. Work is serious. It is not meant to be particularly enjoyable. It is what we are paid to do and probably wouldn't want to do unless we were paid. Play is secondary. It is carefully confined to weekends, holidays and – characteristically – childhood; that is, to the non-productive corners of existence.

But there is another tradition, one that can be seen as 'aristocratic' or 'bohemian', that doesn't draw a sharp line between work and play. The playful person isn't necessarily a slacker; rather, they add a crucial ingredient to productive labour. The playful person finds a way out of the less fruitful aspects of tradition.

The notion that play itself can be serious was promoted in the mid-20th century by the English psychoanalyst Donald Winnicott, who specialised in working with children who were encountering difficulties in their family lives. Winnicott noticed how, in stressful situations, children sometimes react by being 'too good' – that is, very cautious. They feel that they can't risk making a mistake. Yet when a child is being playful, they are liberated from the fear of error. They can try out an idea and it doesn't matter if it's a bit crazy. What if I were in charge of the world? What would I do? What if a lion could speak? What would it say to me?

Beyond the surface impossibility, the child is practising opening its mind to alternative realities. This is a significant skill. Many big ideas in adult life begin as 'what if' thoughts, and we need a constant supply of playful fancies if we are to hit upon new and serious avenues.

The enemy of play is fear. The problem with fearful people isn't that they don't work, but that their work can't be original. Another way of thinking of fearful people is that they start off as overly 'good' children. They do their homework on time; their writing is neat; they keep their bedroom tidy; they are often shy; they want to help their parents; they use their brakes when cycling down a hill. Because they don't pose many immediate problems, we tend to assume that all is well with 'good' children. They aren't the target for particular concern – that goes to the kids who are spray painting graffiti on the underpass. People imagine that the 'good' children are fine because they do everything that is expected of them. And that, of course, is precisely the problem.

The secret sorrows and future difficulties of the good child begin with their need for excessive compliance. The good child isn't good because, by a quirk of nature, they have no inclination to be anything else. They are good because they have no other option. Their goodness is a necessity rather than a choice. Many good children are good out of love for a depressed, harassed parent who makes it clear they can't cope with any more complications or difficulties. Or maybe the child is good in order to soothe a violently angry parent who could become catastrophically frightening at any sign of less-than-perfect conduct. Or perhaps the parent was very busy and distracted; only by being very good could the child hope to gain a sliver of their interest. All this repression of more challenging emotions, although it produces short-term pleasant obedience, stores up a huge amount of difficulty in later life.

Practised educators and parents should spot signs of exaggerated seriousness and politeness and treat them as the danger they are. The good child becomes a keeper of too many secrets and an appalling communicator of unpopular but important things. They say lovely words, they are experts in satisfying the expectations of their audiences, but their real thoughts and feelings stay buried and then generate psychosomatic symptoms, twitches, sudden outbursts and sulphurous bitterness.

The sickness of the good child is that they have no experience of other people being able to tolerate their badness. They have missed out on a vital privilege accorded to the healthy child; that of being able to display playful, envious, greedy, egomaniacal sides and yet be tolerated and loved nevertheless.

At work, the good adult has problems too. They can't play. As a child, they followed the rules; never made trouble and took care not to annoy anyone. But following the rules won't get you very far in adult life. Almost everything that is interesting, worth doing or important will meet with a degree of opposition. A brilliant idea will always disappoint certain people – and yet be worth holding on to. The good child is condemned to career mediocrity and sterile people-pleasing. Being properly mature involves a frank, unfrightened relationship with one's playfulness, complexity and ambition. It involves accepting that not everything that makes us happy will please others or be honoured as especially 'nice' by society – but that it can be important to explore and hold on to it nevertheless. The desire to be good is one of the loveliest things in the world, but in order to have a genuinely good life, we may sometimes need to learn to play – and play naughtily.

17
Purpose

One of the most unsettling aspects of work is that we don't appear to do it solely, and sometimes even principally, for money. We are liable to harbour a far stranger, more demanding ambition: for work that can provide us with 'purpose'. We hunger for this 'purpose' quite as much as we crave status or enrichment, and will often not give our best until we have located it. It is because of purpose that a nurse or an oboe player might give up the chance to afford a spacious home, or that a soldier might – for a relatively modest salary – sacrifice his or her life. Conversely, an absence of purpose might cause an extremely well-paid professional in financial services to resign and fall into a necessary, cathartic depression.

Purposeful work can be defined as any activity that impacts positively on another's life, either by reducing suffering or increasing pleasure. This can encompass everything from the life-saving interventions of the cardiac surgeon to the seductive efforts of a pastry chef or Anatolian rug weaver.

In truth, the vast majority of jobs contribute to the welfare of others in some way. Only a very few are properly devoid of purpose (a career devoted to making fake remedies for hair loss or cancer, perhaps, or one encouraging those on low incomes to gamble more), but a great many are in the odd position of being purposeful, yet not feeling purposeful.

The problem is particularly rife in the modern age because of the scale and tempo ushered in by the Industrial Revolution. Most work now takes place within gigantic organisations engaged in large, complicated and slow-moving projects. Therefore, it can be hard to derive, on a daily basis, any tangible sense of having improved anyone else's life. We are far from the pleasures of small business which – however challenging they are in reality – are at the centre of our fantasies of productive labour. The customer and the end product are, in the mega-structures of modernity, too far away. We can't easily reassure oneself of our worth when we are only a single unit among a twenty-thousand strong team on four continents pushing forward a project that might be ready in five years. It isn't a coincidence that football is – comparatively – so much better at holding our attention: it is limited to twenty-two players and one ball operating on a single pitch for ninety minutes. If modern work were translated into this idiom, it would unfold on eighteen pitches with twenty-two balls and eight hundred players for thousands of days. It is no wonder that we sometimes lose the thread or can't muster the enthusiasm to get out of bed.

Take this as an example: this morning, we need to discuss some data with the market research team, but the key person is away. There's a conference call to confirm that the client is happy with the approach, but it emerges that they can only give a provisional assent; they need more time to check with all their stakeholders on the project (and even then it will turn out that someone is pushing for a few important revisions). Then, after eight rounds of discussion, the main person who was supporting the venture moves to another role. Their successor has a different point of view; there are some tricky legal issues that need attention, and the company tax implications are unclear. We will need to get more support from a slightly sceptical senior partner. It can seem as if work is primarily an arena of exasperation and delay.

When he was trying to define the nature of good drama, the ancient Greek philosopher Aristotle concentrated on what makes a story maximally comprehensible. He thought that the story should unfold quickly in one place, with only a few clearly described main characters. The action shouldn't be very complicated; and everything should unfold in a logical way. There should be an obvious starting point, a decisive, definite ending and a direct route between the two. He was mapping out the ideal pace at which we would like our own lives to unfold.

In reality, this is very far from how things usually go. The drama of our working endeavours might have dozens or hundreds of characters in them, many of whom we don't really know, or whose motives we never properly understand. We can't quite tell when things are complete. Maybe this is just a pause while people regroup; maybe it is truly over? Maybe we are still really at the start of a bigger process. Or maybe we are heading in the wrong direction and are getting further away from the hoped-for endpoint. Our minds naturally demand a clearer and more satisfying pattern than is provided by the messy processes of reality. Frustration, disappointment and impatience are some of the names we can give to the divergence between the ideal model and the way things actually unfold.

Reminding ourselves of the necessary slowness of work counteracts an unfortunate side effect of an unintentional kindness on the part of businesses: concealing from the user the labour that went into creating the goods and services we enjoy. Because we tend to encounter only the final result – after all the difficulties have been resolved – it is easy to give ourselves an unduly streamlined, simplified and pleasant picture of how it came about. Impatience is not so much frustration at things taking a long time in any absolute sense, but the feeling that they are taking longer than they should. Sometimes this may truly be the case. But often the problem is not so much the time things take as our assumptions about how long they are supposed to take. We bring this tight timeframe to bear primarily out of ignorance. It is because we don't fully understand the nature of the task that we do not budget accurately for time.

The danger that a sense of purpose will – more or less unfairly – disappear from our lives places an onus on modern companies to work hard at unlocking the logic of what they are up to. Some jobs do not require any particular effort to tease out their purpose. The relevance (and therefore the worth) of a life in the army is easy to grasp. Everything, from cleaning shoes to crawling under barbed-wire assault courses, has obvious reasons behind it. But other fields offer a minimal sense of their purpose. A packaging supervisor in Malmö might not have much idea of how their work (ordering pallets and stacking them in a three-storey warehouse) fits in with the activities of a geochemist in Ghana who compares activated alumina with indigenous laterite, or with the concerns of a legal expert currently staying in the Alvear Palace Hotel in Buenos Aires and reporting to a steering committee in New York about the implications of proposed revisions to Section 14 of the Argentine

Mining Code. These occupations might well be contributing to the same rather noble cause, only not a cause that their protagonists can quite remember day to day.

Part of the answer to our feelings of disconnection and disorientation lies in a discipline at the heart of culture: storytelling. As the complexity and scale of organisations increases, so we need to learn how to arrange a disparate selection of events into a master narrative that can lend them coherence and remind us of how we fit into a purposeful whole.

A company's 'story' has a lot in common with a large, layered novel. One can imagine a company novel that would begin with a description of someone accessing a bank account in Salzburg. The next moment, we would be in a restaurant in the Wan Chai District of Hong Kong, where a deal is being hammered out to transfer crates to Dubai. Then the focus would be on a meeting taking place in a basement in Whitehall, where regulations for consumer goods are being discussed between ministers and civil servants. Then would come a section set in a call centre in Phoenix, closely followed by a scene in a nursery in Seattle. But rather than hopeless confusion, the point would be to reveal how these apparently random incidents were in fact profoundly interconnected and pointing to a grand overarching goal: the creation of a new IT system for an office in Munich or a project to increase the flow rate of a pump production line in southern Spain. Ideally, every large company would have storytellers on the payroll.

Jan Vermeer painted his famous milkmaid at work in 1657. Today, it is one of the most valuable paintings in the world. Some five

The artist portrays with great tenderness and respect a woman engaged in what might seem a very humble occupation. __Johannes Vermeer, *The Milkmaid*, c.1660.

million visitors come to see it at the Rijksmuseum in Amsterdam every year. However, despite the prestige of the artwork, the moment being depicted could not be more ordinary.

It is only because of the skill and humanity of the artist that the activity unfolds as purposeful. Vermeer looks deep into his milkmaid's work and finds in it an occupation that draws on humility, patience and a respect for procedure. Vermeer understands that a good life needs many things, and that milk (and cream and cheese and yoghurt) occupy a secure place on a very long list in which every element is – once we have learnt to appreciate it – indelibly connected with others in a continuous chain of purpose.

More than ever, we need the generosity of the artistic eye to render the purpose of work more visible to us as employees and to the world; then the logic of our days might be less elusive and our disheartened moments less sapping and severe.

18
Resilience

One of the characteristic flaws of our minds is to exaggerate how fragile we are; to assume that life would become impossible far more easily than it actually would. We imagine that we could not live without a certain kind of income or status or health; that it would be a disaster not to have a certain kind of relationship, house or job.

This natural tendency of the mind is constantly stoked by life in commercial society, which adds to our sense of the number of things that should be considered necessities rather than luxuries. This kind of society goes to extraordinary lengths to make us feel that we really do need to go skiing once a year, have heated car seats, fly Business class, own the same kind of watch as a famous architect and a jumbo-sized fridge, and lay claim to lots of friends, a perfectly muscular physique and a loving, kind, sex-filled relationship.

Our core needs are much simpler than this. We could manage perfectly well with very much less, not just in terms of possessions but in every aspect of our lives. It's not that we should want to live like this, it's simply that we could. We could cope quite well with being rather poor, not being very popular, not having a very long life and with living alone. To offer an extreme instance, we could even cope with being dead; it happens all the time. But we forget our resilience in the face of the risks we contend with. The cumulative effect of our innocence is to make us timid. Our lives become dominated by a fear of losing, or never getting, things that we could in fact manage without.

The ancient Roman philosopher Seneca had great success running what we would now call a venture capital firm. He owned

_____ Our lives become dominated by a fear of losing, or never getting, things that we could in fact manage without.

beautiful villas and magnificent furniture. But he made a habit of regularly sleeping on the floor of an outhouse, eating only stale bread and drinking lukewarm water. He regularly reminded himself that it wouldn't be so bad to lose nearly everything, in order to free himself of nagging worries of catastrophe. This realisation gave him great confidence. He never worried so much about what might happen if a deal went wrong. At the very worst, he'd only be back on the kitchen floor next to the dog basket, and this was something he knew he could cope with.

Seneca was initiating an important move. By continually renewing our acquaintance with our own resilience – that is, with our ability to manage even if things go badly (getting sacked, a partner walking out, a scandal that destroys our social life, an illness) – we can be braver. We grasp that the dangers we face are almost never as great as our skittish imaginations might suggest.

In an ideal world, our culture would stop presenting us with rags-to-riches stories. It would instead do something far kinder and more conducive to the kind of courageous entrepreneurial optimism our societies currently try to foster so ineptly. We would hear of non-tragic riches-to-rags stories; stories in which people lost money, partners and social standing but ended up coping rather well with their new lives. We would see them moving out of the penthouse into a humble cottage and having quite a nice time tending to a small flowerbed and discovering tinned food. Our culture would not necessarily recommend such scenarios, but it would lessen the grip of the misplaced fears that might hold us back from trying and succeeding at our bolder moves.

19
Self-awareness

When asked to sum up the essential counsel of philosophy, Socrates – widely thought of as the wisest man in the ancient world – was said to have responded with just two words: 'Know yourself.'

If self-awareness is central to a wise and fulfilled life, it is because it helps render our peculiar minds somewhat less unpredictable, perplexing and unreliable in their operations. With a measure of self-awareness, we learn to know which of our many, often contradictory, feelings and plans we might trust. We can be a little more sceptical around our first impulses and less puzzled by the ebb and flow of our moods. We understand where some of our feelings have come from and what might be driving our convictions and our longings. We have a way to explain our antics to others, offering them reassurance, warning and more eloquent pleas for forgiveness. Self-awareness can correct the customary vagueness of our thoughts, converting our prejudices into arguments and our hunches into communicable ideas. It enables us to keep a record of some of what flows through our consciousness and to exert a measure of control over our emotions. Not least, knowing ourselves renders us slightly more interesting to be around, for we can better communicate what it feels like to be us.

Unfortunately, knowing ourselves is also one of the hardest tasks we face. Not only do our minds seldom have any desire to look in on themselves, they lack the aptitude to do so. Even a generous witness would need to conclude that introspection was neither a natural nor a spontaneous gift of our species. Even if we are in theory committed to looking within, we cannot simply open a hatch to find ourselves.

We can only get a sense of who we are obliquely. We have to surmise who we might be, but can never find ourselves as we might a stable, prominent landmark. We are not destinations or coherent beings. We miss most of the obscure and transient sensations travelling through our consciousness.

Our visual appearance misleads us in this respect; from the outside, we seem much more whole and complete than we ever are to ourselves. Within, we are a series of fragmented impressions careering through a ceaseless, rapidly flowing river of consciousness. We're closer to scudding clouds, or confused, dancing flames, than we are to the apparently coherent person staring back at us in the mirror.

We are assailed at every moment by vast numbers of sensations and fragmentary insights that we have no time, strength or will to decode. The bulk of what we carry within our minds is never fully acknowledged, unpicked or truly felt. This isn't merely a coincidence. Much of what it would be useful to know about ourselves is potentially disturbing. If we were to pinpoint it accurately and realise its significance, we might discover that some of our feelings were at odds with our values or that some of our anxieties might signal a need to make significant changes to our lives. As these potential implications start to come into view, our inner censor, motivated by a desire for calm rather than growth, becomes alarmed. A vigilant part of the self is agitated, distracts us and muddles our train of thought, blocking the progress we were starting to make towards understanding ourselves. Most of what we are escapes us.

No one intends for this to happen, but somewhere in our

Somewhere in our childhood, our trajectory towards emotional maturity will almost certainly have been impeded.

childhood, our trajectory towards emotional maturity will almost certainly have been impeded. Even if we have been sensitively cared for and lovingly handled, we can be counted upon not to pass through our young years without sustaining some form of deep psychological injury – what we can term a *primal wound*.

Childhood opens us up to emotional damage in part because, unlike all other living things, *Homo sapiens* has an inordinately long and structurally claustrophobic pupillage. A foal can stand up thirty minutes after it is born. By the age of eighteen, a human will have spent around 25,000 hours in the company of its parents. A female grouper mother will unsentimentally dump up to 100 million eggs a year in the sandy banks off the north Atlantic seaboard, then swim away, never to see a single one of her offspring again. Even the blue whale, the largest animal on the planet, is sexually mature and independent by the age of five.

But humans dither and linger. It can be a year till we take our first steps and two before we can speak a whole sentence. It is close to two decades before we are categorised as adults. In the meantime, we are at the mercy of that highly peculiar and distorting institution we call home, and its even more distinctive overseers, our parents.

Across the long summers and winters of childhood, we are intimately shaped by the ways of the big people around us: we come to know their favourite expressions, their habits, how they respond to a delay, the way they address us when they're cross. We know the atmosphere of home on a bright July morning and in the afternoon downpours of mid-April. We memorise the textures of the carpets and the smells of the clothes cupboard. As adults, we can still recall the taste of a particular biscuit we liked to eat after school and know intimately the tiny sounds a mother or father will make as they concentrate on an article in the newspaper. We can return to our original home for a holiday when we are parents ourselves and find, despite our car, responsibilities and lined faces, that we are eight years old again.

During our elongated gestation, we are at first, in a physical sense, completely at the mercy of our caregivers. We are so frail, we could be tripped up by a twig; the family cat is like a tiger. We need help crossing the road, putting on our coat, writing our name.

But our vulnerability is as much emotional. We can't begin to understand our strange circumstances: who we are; where our feelings come from; why we're sad or furious; how our parents fit into the wider scheme of things; why they behave as they do. We necessarily take what the big people around us say as an inviolable truth; we can't help but exaggerate our parents' role on the planet. We are condemned to be enmeshed in their attitudes, ambitions, fears and inclinations. Our upbringing is always particular and peculiar.

As children, we can brush off very little of it. We are without a skin. If a parent shouts at us, the foundations of the earth tremble. We can't tell that some of the harsh words weren't perhaps entirely meant, or had their origins in a difficult day at work or are the reverberations of the adult's own childhood. It feels as if an all-powerful, all-knowing giant has decided, for certain good (if as yet unknown) reasons, that we are to be annihilated.

Nor can we understand, when a parent goes away for the weekend, or relocates to another country, that they didn't leave us because we did something wrong or because we are unworthy of their love, but because even adults aren't always in control of their own destinies.

If parents are in the kitchen raising their voices, it can seem as though these two people must hate one another inordinately. To children, an overheard altercation (with slammed doors and swear words) may feel catastrophic, as though everything safe will imminently disintegrate. There is no evidence in the child's grasp that arguments are a normal part of relationships and that a couple may be committed to a life-long union and at the same time forcefully express a wish that the other go to hell.

Children are equally helpless before the distinctive theories of the parents. They can't understand that an insistence that they not mix with another family from school, or that they follow particular dress codes, or hate a given political party, or worry about dirt or being less than two hours early for a flight represent a very partial understanding of priorities and reality. Children don't have a job. They can't go elsewhere. They have no extended social network. Even when things are going right, childhood is an open prison.

As a result of the peculiarities of the early years, we become distorted and unbalanced. Things within us start to develop in odd directions. We find we can't easily trust, or need to keep any sign of dirt at bay or become unusually scared around people who raise their voices. No one needs to do anything particularly shocking, illegal, sinister or wicked to us for very serious distortions to unfold. The causes of our primal wound are rarely outwardly dramatic, but its effect can be momentous and long-lasting. Such is the fragility of childhood, nothing outwardly appalling need have happened to us for us to wind up profoundly scrambled.

We know this point from tragedy. In the tragic tales of the Ancient Greeks, it is not enormous errors and slips that unleash drama: it is the tiniest, most innocent mistakes. Terrible consequences unfurl from seemingly minor starting points. Our emotional lives are similarly tragic in structure. Everyone around us may have been trying to do their best for us as children, yet we have ended up as adults nursing major hurts that ensure we are much less than we might be.

A key aspect of self-awareness is to become conscious of our transferences. Transference is a psychological phenomenon whereby a situation in the present elicits from us a response cobbled together from our childhood experiences to meet a threat that, at the time, we were too vulnerable, immature and inexperienced to cope with properly. We draw upon an old defence mechanism to respond to what feels like a familiar menace.

In most of our pasts, when our powers of comprehension and control were not properly developed, we faced difficulties so great that our capacities for poise and trust suffered grievous damage. In relation to certain issues, we were warped. We grew up preternaturally nervous, suspicious, hostile, sad, closed, furious or touchy – and are at risk of becoming so once again whenever life puts us in a situation that evokes our earlier troubles.

The unconscious mind is slow to realise that things have changed in the outer world and is sadly quick to mistake one person for another, twenty years ago for now, seeming to judge only by the crudest of correspondences.

Transference generally happens without us knowing. We think we are responding to the present while being guided by a pattern from the past. We carry years behind us that we have forgotten about and that we aren't in a position to explain to others in a manner that would win us sympathy and understanding. We can easily come across as mean or mad.

The concept of transference provides a vantage point on some of the most frustrating behaviours that any of us ever generate. It allows us to feel sympathy for other people where we might have only felt irritation. A wiser culture would teach us that transference is normal. Recognising that one is doing it oneself is not an admission of unusual idiocy; it's an instance of mature self-knowledge.

It does not lie within any of our remits to be entirely content – or sane. There are powerful reasons why we lack an even keel. We have complex histories, we are heading towards the ultimate catastrophe, we are vulnerable to devastating losses; love will never go wholly well, the gap between our hopes and our reality will be huge. In the circumstances, it does not make sense to aim for sanity. We should focus instead on the goal of achieving a wise, knowledgeable and self-possessed relationship with our manifold insanities, or what we might term 'sane insanity'. The sane insane differ from the simply insane by virtue of the honest and accurate grasp they have on what is not right with them. They may not be wholly balanced, but they don't have the additional folly of insisting on their normality. They can admit with good grace, and no particular loss of dignity, that they are extremely peculiar in myriad ways. They do not go out of their way to hide from us what they get up to in the night, in their sad moments, when anxiety strikes or during attacks of envy. At their best they can be drily funny about the tragedy of being human. They lay bare the fears, doubts, longings, desires and habits that don't belong to the story we like to tell ourselves about sanity. They don't make ready confessions to let themselves off the hook or to be eccentric. They realise the unreasonableness of expecting to be reasonable all the time. They warn others as far as possible in advance of what being around them might involve, and apologise promptly for their failings as soon as they manifest themselves. They offer their friends and companions accurate maps to their craziness, which is about the most generous thing one can do for anyone who has to endure us.

The sane insane among us are not a special category of the mentally unwell: they represent the most evolved possibility for a mature human being.

20
Supportiveness

The wise office does not make the error of supposing that there could ever be a psychologically 'normal' human being or lasting, complete harmony across all departments. It knows full well, and is undisturbed by the idea, that we are all distinctively odd, anxious and only just holding it together. This is wholly to be expected and in no way shameful. The wise office has no interest in the fanciful and cruel notion that things could ever be 'professional' at all times. It recognises the concept of professionalism for what it is: a conspiracy to persuade us that we might be more level-headed than any of us actually are.

The aim of the wise office is to mitigate the worst of our psychological frailties, not to deny that these exist. This is supportiveness. The process begins with a blanket admission, embedded within the company culture, that everyone will experience periods of mental volatility. Succumbing to terror, starting to cry, falling into despair aren't anomalies; they are what happens when talented people get together and try to do difficult things.

A good company reveres more than just the strengths of its people; it is ready to remember, and make accommodations for, all their peculiarities of spirit. The good office gives itself unalarming accounts of what is going on when an individual is preternaturally adrift, worried or thoughtful. They are like this not because they are misguided, weak-willed or selfish, but because they are – like everyone – slightly broken.

At a collective level, we have given ourselves unfrightened accounts of what's going on when teenagers sit moodily staring out of the window and don't answer when someone asks them to pass the salt. We know these young people aren't heading for a life of delinquency; we can remain confident that a reconciliation with the demands of the world will emerge. We should expect analogous periods of confusion and loss of direction to punctuate the lives of every employee. The good office knows that sanity simply isn't possible for any of us all the time.

Because its culture recognises and normalises error, the wise office is correspondingly always open to learning, taking constant care to instruct and guide. Learning is not a process that ended with a university degree. The wise office accepts that pointing out to every individual – with infinite tact – the many ways in which they are imperfect is not a violation of their dignity, but the foundation of care; even of a certain kind of love.

At the same time, it knows that we operate with an unhelpful notion of love which suggests that the principal marker of kindness is the capacity to accept another person in their totality, with all their good and bad sides – particularly their bad sides. To love someone is – according to the prevailing romantic philosophy – to love them as they are, with no wish to alter them. But there is another more workable and mature philosophy of love available in the philosophy of the Ancient Greeks, who recognised that love is first and foremost an admiration for the good sides and the strengths of another human being and will therefore entail a commitment to a journey of education around everything that may be less than perfect.

Part of what it means to deepen love is, for the Greeks, to want to teach and to be taught. When they teach each other uncomfortable truths, people are not giving up on love, they are trying to be true to it: to encourage someone to grow into the best version of themselves. In the wise office, lessons are not immediately heard as criticism; they are accepted as belonging to a process of chiselling at our troublesome personalities. Endorsement of all our existing failings is not love.

The wise office knows that acquiring knowledge can be bitter. It is therefore interested in making lessons sweet. The Basilica of the Fourteen Holy Helpers is a church in Bavaria that was finished in 1772. It contains some highly relevant lessons for the process of teaching. The Basilica's sponsor, the Catholic Church, wanted to encourage its followers to take all sorts of ideas on board: being compassionate and caring; acknowledging the extent of Jesus's sacrifice; being humble before the perfections of an omnipotent god.

But the Church was also keen to avoid a technique that they'd been trying for centuries and that hadn't worked well: terrifying and guilt-tripping people into learning. In this part of southern Germany, for a time at least, they settled on a different, much more intelligent, way of teaching. They weren't going to talk about hell and damnation any more; they would attempt to charm and seduce people into being good. They wouldn't nag, issue stern warnings or upbraid people for being selfish. Instead, they asked their architect, Balthasar Neumann, to use every possible means to persuade people to develop their characters through excitement, pleasure, awe and delight.

Interior of the Basilica of the
Fourteen Holy Helpers, Bavaria.
The beauty of this lavish setting
was a way for the Catholic
Church to make its teachings
palatable; seductive, even.

The interlocking domes and vaults of the basilica are exceptionally beautiful, inducing a mood of lightness and vitality. Looking up at the ceiling, one feels in the presence of an embodiment of happiness. The building is splendid – but for a reason. It knows we need a lot of encouragement to grow. The wise office, too, accepts that there are few more serious tasks than to overcome the many obstacles to getting important ideas into another person's head.

The wise office is ready for things not to go smoothly. Although we may associate good collaboration with agreement and harmony, moments of sharp, even bitter, disagreement are just as much a part of what we should expect. This possibility was memorably explored by the German philosopher Hegel. In his work of 1807, *The Phenomenology of Spirit*, Hegel concluded that many of our most important ideas emerge through a violent collision of, and eventual reconciliation between, competing notions, each of which possesses a part, but not the whole of, the truth. Hegel encourages us not to be too alarmed by clashes of ideas. The ideal collaboration involves tension, profound disagreements and divergences in outlook. It generally takes three moves before the right balance on any issue can be found; a process that Hegel named the 'dialectic'.

In his own lifetime, Hegel pointed out that governments had eventually improved, but only after a succession of extraordinarily painful steps. The flawed, stifling, unfair 18th-century system of traditional inherited monarchy had been abolished by the French Revolution, whose founding fathers had wanted to give a voice to the majority. But what should have been the peaceful birth of representative government had ended up in the anarchy and chaos of The Terror. This in turn had led to the emergence of Napoleon, who had restored order and ensured opportunity for talent and ability, but who had then overreached himself and turned into a military brute, tyrannising the rest of Europe and trampling on the liberty he had professed to love. Eventually, the modern 'balanced constitution' had emerged, an arrangement that more sensibly balanced popular representation with the rights of minorities. However, this resolution had taken at least forty years and incalculable agony to reach.

Hegel asked us not to be surprised: progress is by nature slow and troubled. He added that what happens in history will also occur in individual lives. We too learn slowly and with massive over-corrections. Take our emotional lives: we might, in our twenties, have been with someone who was so intense we felt suffocated. We therefore freed ourselves and took up with someone cooler and more reserved, but they could eventually also have become oppressive in their distance. By our early fifties we might finally be getting this aspect of our lives more or less right. It may seem like the most appalling waste of time, but, Hegel insists, the painful stepping from error to error is almost inevitable, and something we must expect and reconcile ourselves to in history as much as in our private and professional lives.

For all their many flaws and irritating characteristics, we need teams, because virtues need to be counterbalanced and individual weaknesses compensated for. Our acceptance of the dignity and role of collaboration should be founded on a basic recognition of the fact that big tasks demand a symphony of different skills. We can develop a respect for some of the off-putting people on our team when we understand that their irritating sides are connected with skills we lack and need. We should be spared any pressure to be friends with them; we can just be glad they are working with us. Successful collaborators should be wary of offices with too many like-minded spirits. They know that good teams (teams that can take on complicated challenges by synthesising varied strengths) will have to contain people who don't temperamentally like one another very much.

A sullen resentment of those in power is as widespread in most offices as it is quietly corrosive. In the arts, the attitude finds itself most cogently expressed in caricature. Most of us learnt about caricature at school, where we were all natural geniuses at identifying the weaknesses and failings of those who had robbed us of our liberty. The physics teacher was a bit disorganised, wore a jacket with strangely thin lapels and occasionally missed certain portions of his face when shaving. His name was Mr Acevedo, which of course became Mr Avocado. It can be rather gratifying to think ill of the powerful.

In the early 19th century, the English caricaturist James Gillray portrayed Charles James Fox – then leader of the Opposition – as a villainous-looking halfwit (he is standing centre right, slightly bowing, with a sword at his side and looking shifty, next to his wife, who carries a fan). Everyone in the picture has their faults brilliantly highlighted. Many look unbearably smug. The individual in a crimson jacket bowing practically to the ground and looking

There is great satisfaction to be had in portraying the powerful as fools. Satirist James Gillray's depiction of the English political scene, 1804.

L'ASSEMBLÉE NATIONALE ; _ or _ Grand Cooperative Meeting at St. Ann's Hill. _ Respectfully Dedicated to the admirers of a Broad Bottom'd Administration

farcically obsequious is William Grenville, who became prime minister a few years after the print appeared.

Gillray was regarded as the greatest satirist of his age, but by modern standards he was operating within a culture in which the traditions of respect and deference were still strong. In the modern world, however, cynicism towards the powerful has become all-encompassing. More or less everyone who arrives in a position of leadership or authority may be resented. It is to our collective credit that we find it unacceptable for the strong to mock the weak. Yet there are some complications to an age in which it is routine for the weak to resent the strong.

Caricature misses things. Fox certainly had some weaknesses (he liked gambling, he had multiple mistresses, he used to spit on the carpet), but he was also a major advocate of progressive ideas, the abolition of the slave trade and the evolution of political rights among them. Gillray didn't care about discovering Fox as a human being; there was too much fun to be had outlining him as a freak. But wilfully misunderstanding people cuts us off from a host of useful and consoling insights.

The central discovery is that the unpleasantness of those in senior roles tends to come not from evil, as we only too easily suppose, but anxiety, as we are far less inclined to imagine. It is frightening to head an organisation. The possibilities for disaster are multiple and constant. The risks of humiliation are never far away and retribution for errors can be swift and brutal. It is unsurprising that leaders frequently seem impatient, sarcastic and brusque: they are in a cold panic. If they revealed their distress more obviously – if they wept, looked terrified or simply explained what it was like to be them – we might behave more gently and less cynically. Yet it is precisely their distress that prevents them from revealing their humanity and gives rise to their misleadingly stern and unfortunate disguises.

One of the key moves of psychoanalysis has been to reveal the extent of the trouble children have in understanding that a difficult mood exhibited by a parent may not be about them. When Dad is shouting, the child naturally tends to imagine that it must be her fault, even if the real cause is a challenge at work or a difficulty in the parental relationship. It feels odd to accept that those who are hurting us may not be harbouring any ill will towards us. Periodic reminders that there can be off-stage causes for other people's bad moods is critical when navigating our way through life. Learning not to take it personally is not a last counsel of despair; it is usually an accurate assessment of what is going on in the minds of those who have upset us.

Even more strangely, on occasion, the senior person who looks so hateful may have appealing sides in parts of their life we don't see. The character who seems so irritable in meetings may be forgiving and gentle with the hospice residents she works with on weekends. The king, so ruthless in the throne room, may be an amiable playmate in the nursery.

The ideal company would not preach to its employees about the beauty of motivation. It would manage morale by presenting them with helpful theories of human nature, continually reminding them of the adult truth about how relatively decent people can, when worried, behave with contempt for the feelings of others. At the same time, it would help managers to see the virtue of admitting to weakness rather than risk being mistaken for cold-hearted bullies; we can forgive a lot when we know that people act principally out of fear rather than cruelty.

The wise office recognises that emotional intelligence cannot only reside off-stage, inert. It helps to have a living representative within the office itself. At the high points of religious culture in Europe, the great houses – which were approximations of what we would now call businesses – regularly employed priests and chaplains. These guardians of the spiritual side of existence would eat with families and their staff, write sermons, deliver advice, listen to the regrets of the dying and inspire the young to virtue. Louis XIV of France hired Jacques-Bénigne Bossuet to guide the inner lives of his court at Versailles. Bossuet sometimes gave quite serious public rebukes to the king from the pulpit, something made possible by his clerical status; no other adviser would have been able to get away with this.

The English poet John Donne was the private chaplain to the Earl of Carlisle and accompanied him on an important diplomatic embassy to the German States and France (1618–1620). The philosopher Johann Gottfried Herder was a Lutheran pastor employed by a succession of noble families in Russia and Germany. These economically and politically significant organisations known as noble families regarded spiritual support and advice as crucial, not just for the head of the family firm but for the heirs, up-and-coming leaders and ordinary workers. The priest didn't just undertake religious ceremonies (which would only take a few hours a week); he sat with the team at dinner, talking through their psychological troubles and helping them address their central worries and decisions.

The wise modern office should learn the best lessons from cultural history. Alongside IT and marketing, finance and catering, the wise office would employ a therapist, the modern version of the priestly figure, sitting at lunch and in the CEO's office, circulating among the workstations and in the communal kitchen. One would take to the therapist the grievances and sorrows that are currently seldom addressed in a work context. Currently, the only place where we dare to be honest – and then often in the clumsiest ways – is in relationships. At work, we are essentially avoidant; we give up on people, suffer in silence or change jobs. The price of this miscommunication is enormous. The office air is dense with information that, if it were made concrete, could transform the environment. We lack the emotional skill to frame issues in ways that don't humiliate and that don't portray us as vindictive, self-pitying or mean. In this context, the therapist becomes a kind of diplomat – a go-between – the skilful and professional ambassador of vitally important knowledge.

The wise office promises us something remarkable: that work won't just be a place that drains our personalities, but could teach us about ourselves and our emotional failings and give us skills to address them that we could take back to our private lives. Our labour would not then merely be something we unfortunately had to do; it would play a part in our emotional development. It would be one of the places where we learnt the maturity we need in all areas of our lives, including our homes. Via the experience of work, we might develop some crucial abilities: to understand our weaknesses; to communicate our feelings and wishes calmly, to learn to listen to uncomfortable views; and to be patient with fiddly things.

In the late 18th and early 19th centuries, influential writers, artists and philosophers developed the view that the kind of work most people do – management, sales, manufacturing, logistics – is detrimental to the human spirit. If we were sketching a utopia, we would not create a society in which people didn't have to work. It would be one in which more and more people had the chance to acquire, via their work, the emotional talents that would be useful across the whole of their lives. Being a good employee shouldn't be that different from being that truly important thing, a good person. Learning a trade shouldn't just be a means to acquire money; it should involve a coded lesson in growing up.

The School of Life
for Business

These essays are thought pieces based on the topics covered by The School of Life's Business unit.

We work with businesses to help employees function better together – to form more engaged teams, be more productive, dynamic, and work together in more innovative and entrepreneurial ways.

For each of the twenty emotional skills we teach, we provide a precisely designed workshop delivered by a world class faculty. We provide suggested learning-journeys or can tailor one for the needs of particular organisations.

For more information, see:
www.theschooloflife.com/business

List of works

P9
Carl Friedrich H. Werner (1808–94)
The Artist's Studio, Venice, 1855
Watercolour on paper, 62 × 72 cm
Russell-Cotes Art Gallery and Museum,
Bournemouth

P13
Raphael (1483–1520)
*Head of Saint Catherine and Sketches
of Cupids*, c.1507–8
Pen and brown ink over traces of black
chalk, 169 × 279 mm
The Ashmolean Museum, Oxford

P34
Jacob van Ruisdael (1629–82)
The Windmill at Wijk bij Duurstede,
1670
Oil on canvas, 83 × 101 cm
Rijksmuseum, Amsterdam

P37
Agency: Doyle Dane Bernbach
Advertising campaign for Volkswagen
Beetle, introduced 1959

P41
Ben Nicholson (1894–1982)
1935 (white relief), 1935
Painted wood, 101.6 × 166.4 cm
Tate, London

P96
John Singer Sargent (1856–1925)
Lord Ribblesdale, 1902
Oil on canvas, 258.4 × 143.5 cm
The National Gallery, London

P116
Guo Xu (1456–c.1529)
Mi Fu and Elder Brother Rock, 1503
Album leaf; ink and colors on paper,
29.8 × 49.3 cm
Shanghai Museum, Shanghai

P117
Claude Monet (1840–1926)
La Manneporte près d'Etretat, 1886
Oil on canvas, 81.3 × 65.4 cm
The Metropolitan Museum of Art,
New York

P125
Caravaggio (1571–1610)
The Supper at Emmaus, 1601
Oil on canvas, 141 cm × 196.2 cm
National Gallery, London

P151
Johannes Vermeer (1632–1675)
The Milkmaid, c.1660
Oil on canvas, 45.5 × 41 cm
Rijksmuseum, Amsterdam

P171
Basilica of Fourteen Holy
Helpers (altar)
Constructed between 1743 and 1772
Bad Staffelstein, Bavaria

P175
James Gillray (1756–1815)
*L'Assemblée Nationale; —or—Grand
Co-operative Meeting at St. Ann's Hill*,
1804
Etching, hand coloured,
33.4 × 46.4 cm
Library of Congress, Prints & Photo-
graphs Division, LC-USZC4-13054

Picture credits

The **School of Life** is dedicated to developing emotional intelligence – believing that a range of our most persistent problems are created by a lack of self-understanding, compassion and communication. We operate from ten physical campuses around the world, including London, Amsterdam, Seoul and Melbourne. We produce films, run classes, offer therapy and make a range of psychological products. **The School of Life Press** publishes books on the most important issues of emotional life. Our titles are designed to entertain, educate, console and transform.